Collins

Disaster Survival

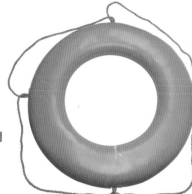

Brian Beard

First published in 2007 by Collins
an imprint of
HarperCollins Publishers
77–85 Fulham Palace Road, London W6 8JB
www.collins.co.uk

Collins is a registered trademark of
HarperCollins Publishers Limited

10 09 08 07
6 5 4 3 2 1

A catalogue record for this book is available from the
British Library

Produced for Collins by Essential Works Ltd
168a Camden Street, London NW1 9PT

ISBN: 978-0-00-724736-3

Colour reproduction by Digital Imaging
Printed and bound by Amadeus s.r.l.

For Essential Works
Editor: Julia Halford
Designer: Michael Gray
Illustrator: Matt Pagett
Proofreader: Dipli Saikia
Indexer: Hazel Bell

This book is proudly printed on paper which contains wood from
well managed forests certied in accordance with the rules of the
Forest Stewardship Council. For more information about FSC,
please visit www.fsc-uk.org.

Contents

3 Terrorism

4 Disease and temperature extremes

5 Dealing with disasters

Damage caused by the Asian tsunami of December 2004.

Introduction

Disaster can strike anywhere, anytime, and
in a multitude of ways. For anyone involved,
as in the Asian tsunami of 2004, the
consequences can be devastating. Survival
can depend upon a combination of factors,
or merely pure luck, but the key phrase has
to be 'preparation through information'.

Forewarned may be forearmed and, while such
preparation cannot nullify damage, it can lessen the
impact upon people and their environment. It may
never happen, but it is better to be prepared. In
1965, when a 'blackout' hit the eastern seaboard
of the United States and plunged 80,000 square
miles of the richest, most powerful nation on the
planet into 13 hours of chaos, how many of the
30 million people affected muttered the phrase
'I wish I had a flashlight'?

Some disasters hit without warning, others,
by the nature of their location, are a case of when,
not if. Whatever the circumstances, there are a
number of contingencies that should be in place
to minimise impact.

Every home and workplace should have a
comprehensive and fully functional survival kit and
first aid kit, and everyone should be able to use the

contents of both. First aid is taught in many educational establishments and all of us should be able to perform the basics. It could save a life – maybe yours.

Sometimes preparation may be enough, but everyone affected by a disaster will need to use common sense as well. It is difficult to quantify common sense – we all have it, in different measures. But how a person reacts to a disaster situation can determine their ability to call upon common sense – as detailed in 'Psychological and emotional reactions to disaster' in Chapter 5.

The people who are successful in surviving are usually those who have reason to live, obvious though that may seem. Survivors have spoken of the stimulation to overcome, provided by thoughts of family, duty, religion, and so on. Survivors also frequently attest to the 'will to live' syndrome and prayer, neither of which should be underestimated. Survival is undeniably a mental state as well as a physical one.

At this point in time, we need to be aware of possible disaster scenarios caused by climate change, nature, man (including terrorists), and disease. This book provides invaluable advice on how to prepare for and what to do if you find yourself in such a situation.

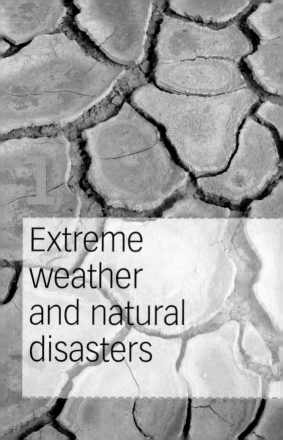

Extreme
weather
and natural
disasters

Blizzards

A blizzard is a storm that produces heavy, blinding snow, resulting in near-zero visibility, deep drifts and dangerous wind-chill. They can cause severe disruption to all means of transport and communication.

PREPARATION

Stay indoors and out of the cold if possible. Weather statistics show that people often fail to heed this obvious advice.

If you must venture outdoors during a blizzard avoid heavy, physical exertion, e.g. shovelling snow, pushing vehicles or attempting to walk great distances through deep snow. The strain from such exertion, in the low temperatures that accompany blizzards, can cause a heart attack. Heavy perspiration can lead to chill and hypothermia.

If at home or work

PREPARATION

Your main concerns will be potential loss of heating, electrical power, telecommunications and a shortage of supplies (including food and safe drinking water).

- Store high-energy foods such as dried fruit, sweets and non-perishable foods (requiring no cooking).
- Fuel for fires – dry wood, coal – needs to be easily accessible.
- Matches for starting a fire should be kept in a convenient location.
- Ensure that your fire source is properly ventilated.
- Make sure that your fire extinguisher and smoke detectors function properly.

SURVIVAL

- If there is no heat, close off any rooms that are not needed.
- Stuff towels, rags or newspaper in gaps under the doors.
- Cover windows, especially at night.
- Keep your body supplied with food; this produces energy for heat.
- Maintain your fluid intake; this helps to prevent dehydration.
- Wear layers of loose-fitting, light, warm clothing – these can then be removed in stages if you begin to overheat.
- Sleep with a hat on and several thin blankets rather than one heavy one.

RESPONSE

- Monitor radio stations and other media sources for news of the storm and base your decision to stay put or venture out on the predicted duration of the severe weather conditions. Listen to the official instructions from the emergency services.
- Stay put unless it is dangerous to do so – i.e. if the building is in danger of collapse.
- Await rescue service response.

Remain in your car until the blizzard passes.

If in a vehicle
PREPARATION
Keep an emergency survival kit (see pp 180–5).

RESPONSE
- If trapped, put on hazard warning lights.
- Attach cloth or rag to aerial/window/sunroof to help you to be seen by rescuers.
- Stay in the car unless safe shelter is visible and accessible or rescuers are in sight. Disorientation occurs rapidly in wind-driven snow and cold.
- If stranded in a remote area do not leave the car until the blizzard passes.

SURVIVAL

- Run the engine for 8–10 minutes each hour, for heating.
- Check that the exhaust is free from obstruction.
- Ensure that the window is slightly open to avoid carbon monoxide poisoning.
- If there is more than one person in the car, huddle together for warmth.
- Rotate sleep spells to ensure someone is awake at all times so rescuers can be alerted.
- If alone, use road maps, seat covers, floor mats, etc, to help generate warmth.
- Exercise occasionally by clapping hands and moving around.
- Do not remain in one position for too long.
- Do not burn anything for heat inside the car. Open fires burn oxygen and give off carbon dioxide, which can cause asphyxiation in a closed vehicle.

If on foot

SURVIVAL

If at all possible, stay in your car or building, but if you have to venture out or are caught on foot:

- Find shelter and attempt to stay dry.
- Cover all exposed body parts.
- If you have no shelter, construct a windbreak

or snow cave for protection from the wind.

- Build a fire for heat and to attract attention.
- Place rocks, bricks or any non-flammable material around the fire to absorb and reflect heat.
- Do not eat snow – it will lower body temperature. Melt it first, then drink the water.

Construct a snow cave for shelter.

Cold

When low temperatures persist below the seasonal norm, it can cause problems for people and their environment – with subsequent health consequences. Much can be done to combat the extreme cold in terms of preparation, given the potential disruption of transport and communications, which can affect food supplies.

Many countries are used to low temperatures and freezing conditions but other areas, whilst having experience of low thermometer readings, may not have the necessary procedures in place.

PREPARATION
- Have your central heating serviced regularly.
- You should have adequate home insulation. Water pipe insulation is crucial (on cold water pipes to prevent freezing; on hot water pipes to prevent heat loss).
- Do not insulate under a cold water tank – a small amount of heat flow will help prevent freezing.
- Check for drafts around doors and windows, and fill gaps.
- Fix plastic sheeting to windows if there is no double glazing.

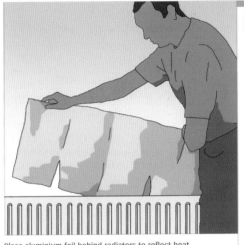

Place aluminium foil behind radiators to reflect heat.

- A hall door curtain will reduce heat loss.
- Fixing cooking foil behind radiators (shiny side facing the room) will reflect heat into the room.
- Unused chimneys should be swept – a good standby if the central heating fails.
- Extreme cold can affect domestic fuel supplies – a camping stove is a good emergency substitute.

Extreme weather and natural disasters

Always keep food in stock, but do not stockpile.

- Ensure that you have at least three days' food supply in the house, but do not stockpile – this can cause panic.
- Check that you have adequate winter clothing.

RESPONSE

- Stay indoors if at all possible.
- Monitor all media outlets for weather and emergency procedure information.
- Check on any neighbours who live alone, especially the elderly.
- Ensure emergency supplies are easily accessible – no power means no electricity.
- Use only one room – an internal room or passage will be easier to heat.
- Regular hot drinks will maintain body heat to fight the cold.
- If freezing pipes are likely, drain water from system and keep as emergency supply; turn off water main and turn taps on to empty pipes.
- If electricity fails, freezers will preserve food for up to 48 hours if the door is kept shut.

IF TRAVEL IS ESSENTIAL

- Ensure that adequate clothing is worn – many light layers are better than one thick layer.
- Mittens are better than gloves as your fingers can share body heat.
- Hats help to prevent heat loss.
- Do not drink alcohol – it will reduce your body temperature.

Droughts

Droughts occur when a long period passes without substantial rainfall, resulting in insufficient water for daily life. A prolonged drought can have a significant economic impact on a community. Increased demand for water may lead to a lack of resources, and a food shortage may occur if agricultural production is damaged or destroyed.

PREPARATION

- Familiarise yourself and your family with official recommendations for voluntary water conservation. This may help to prevent mandatory measures.
- Repair dripping taps – one drop per second equates to 12,274 l (2,700 gal) of wasted water in a year.
- Consider a toilet with a low-volume cistern which uses half the water of older toilets (mandatory in some parts of the USA).
- Store drinking water in the fridge – this will save you having to run the tap until the water gets cold.
- Put a water butt in the garden to collect rain water.

RESPONSE

- Do not waste water – shower instead of bathing.
- Place a bucket in the shower to catch any excess water.
- In the shower conserve water by turning it on to get wet, off to lather, then back on to wash.
- Do not waste water waiting for it to get hot – capture the initial flow for alternative use.
- Do not run the tap continually when cleaning your teeth.
- Do not drink tap water if directed not to by the local authorities; decreasing water levels can

Turn off dripping taps or replace washers, if necessary.

A large stone in the cistern will reduce the volume of water.

result in contamination or pollution from dead animals in the water supply.
- Boil, purify, or buy bottled water if instructed not to drink water directly from the tap.
- Don't flush toilet but ensure that you leave enough water to act as a barrier against smells and possible disease spreading from sewers up the pipes.
- Putting a brick in a cistern is not a good method for reducing the volume of water in your toilet (they can disintegrate and the pieces

can clog pipes and cause damage to internal
parts). Instead, place a 1 l (2 pint) bottle of water
in the cistern to displace the water, or use a
large stone (see opposite).

RECOVERY

A significant factor in recovery for a drought region
is its location in the world. The primary concern is
for the authorities to restore or provide normal
access to safe water for household consumption.
People can help by practising sensible water
conservation:

- Do not pour water down the drain – find another
  use for it.
- Check for leaks, and remedy if found.
- Take short showers.
- Do not run the water continually when brushing
  teeth, washing or shaving.
- Dispose of tissues etc, normally flushed away,
  by another method.
- When hand-washing dishes, fill two bowls: one
  with washing up liquid, one for rinsing.
- Heat water in the microwave rather than
  evaporating via boiling.
- Minimise or eliminate car washing.
- Make sure that your dishwasher and washing
  machine are full when you turn them on.

Dust storms

A dust storm is a strong and violent wind that carries fine particles of dust and debris, and other materials, huge distances. As the debris becomes airborne the fine particles are swirled around by high winds, which have been known to exceed 25 mph. Storm clouds have been recorded reaching a height of 3,048 m (10,000 ft) and moving along a front that can be many miles wide.

Dust storms are not restricted to desert regions – they can happen anywhere there is loose dirt present that can be easily lifted off the ground. The heavier particles usually resettle after a short time but the finer particles, which cause respiratory problems, can remain airborne for many days and have been known to travel thousands of miles. It is not unusual for sand from Saharan dust storms to turn up in the United States and South America.

The conditions conducive to dust storms are usually a result of overgrazing or deforestation, so dust storms should not be confused with sand storms, which are low clouds of moving sand that remain close to the ground. A dust storm usually passes quite quickly, though storms of up to 12 hours have been recorded.

Dust storms can carry debris huge distances.

Preparation for a dust storm can help reduce its impact. However, survival and recovery procedures have to wait for a storm to pass before implementation. Thankfully, the consequences are fairly standard, although they vary in degree.

PREPARATION

A dust storm can arrive with very little warning so it

is important that emergency measures are in place for immediate implementation if you are in an area that is at risk of dust storms. Be aware that the main dangers of a dust storm are reduced visibility, choking particles and flying debris – three good reasons to stay where you are.

- The best advice is: do not go out.
- Dust storms occur after a period of sustained drought. Learn to recognise the signs and monitor media outlets for weather information.
- If a storm is imminent, take shelter immediately.
- Ensure that everyone is indoors, and bring any animals and livestock in as well.
- Tie down or move inside any garden furniture or potential flying debris.
- Protect windows from flying particles with shutters or curtains.
- Plug any gaps around windows and door frames.

RESPONSE
Dust storms can pass as quickly as they arise. Waiting out the storm is the safest course of action. However, if you must go outside during a storm, wear protective gear (especially if you suffer from respiratory problems):

- Goggles will protect your eyes from flying sand and dust.

- Cover your head with a scarf or a bandanna.
- Cover your nose and mouth with a wet cloth to ease breathing.
- A small amount of petroleum jelly under the nostrils will help restrict the drying of the mucous membrane.
- Use lip balm to prevent chaffing.

IF TRAVELLING BY CAR

As dust storms can strike quickly, you might be in your vehicle when one occurs. If a storm cloud is approaching:

- Do not drive into a storm cloud area.
- If it is not possible to pull off a road, drive at a lower speed conducive to conditions. Put all the lights on and sound the horn intermittently.
- If visibility drops below approximately 91.5 m (300 ft), pull over and park up in a safe place if you are able to (away from the road if possible). Never stop and park up on the road.
- Turn off the lights and then engage handbrake. It is important that lights are off as there have been instances of collisions and mass pile-ups because drivers approaching a parked vehicle have taken taillights as a guide and driven off the road.

Heat

Extreme heat occurs when temperatures hover 10°C (50°F) or more above the average high for a region and last for several weeks. The human body can be pushed beyond its limits by excessive heat. Under normal conditions the body's own thermostat produces perspiration that evaporates and cools the body, but in extreme heat and high humidity that evaporation process is slowed and the body then has to work harder to maintain a normal temperature.

The population of urban areas is more at risk because asphalt and concrete store energy longer, and when it's gradually released at night significantly higher temperatures result. This is known as the 'urban island effect'.

PREPARATION

- Install air conditioning and insulate if necessary.
- If air conditioning is already installed, ensure its maintenance is up to date.
- Place temperature reflectors between curtains and windows – such as aluminium foil-covered board – to reflect the heat back outside.

If you have a loft, make sure that it is insulated.

- Attach weather strips to doors and sills to keep cool air in.
- Cover windows exposed to morning/afternoon sun with curtains – outdoor awnings can reduce up to 80 per cent of heat entering a home.

Wear a hat for protection, but avoid too much sun.

RESPONSE

- Stay indoors as much as possible.
- Remain on the lowest floor level if air conditioning is not available (it will be much cooler there).
- Use fans to keep cool air circulating, and make sure that ceiling fan blades are set to drive cool air downwards.

- Slow yourself down. The body cannot function effectively in higher temperatures/humidity.
- Heed your body's early warnings ahead of a heat syndrome. Reduce your activity level and get to a cooler environment.
- Eat less – especially foods that increase metabolic heat production (proteins) and water loss. Well-balanced, light, regular meals are best.
- Drink plenty of water even when not thirsty.
- Limit alcohol intake, as this can dehydrate you.
- Don't get too much sun – sunburn makes heat dissipation more difficult.
- Check on friends and neighbours without air conditioning who may be vulnerable.

RECOVERY

The main effect on the human body of extreme heat involves increased body temperature, causing heat exhaustion and heat stroke (see Hyperthermia, pp 160–3). Recovery from heat stroke can take at least 24 hours and involves rest and re-hydration.

Hurricanes

Hurricanes are severe tropical storms that form in the southern Atlantic, Caribbean, Gulf of Mexico and eastern Pacific. Most hurricanes start as thunderstorms over Africa. They gather heat and energy through contact with warm ocean waters. Evaporation from the seawater increases their power. Hurricanes rotate anti-clockwise around a centre called an 'eye'. Absolutely nothing can stop a hurricane, so the key to survival is preparation.

PREPARATION

When a hurricane watch (notification) is issued:

- Fix hurricane straps to secure your roof.
- If you live near the ocean, inlets, bays, etc, plan to relocate during a hurricane emergency. Storm surge (tidal flooding) is one of the worst killers associated with hurricanes.
- Plan your escape route to a safe area if you have to leave your home.
- Check the time that your escape would take, allowing extra for peak evacuation traffic.
- Mobile homes are not safe places during a hurricane. Always plan relocation.

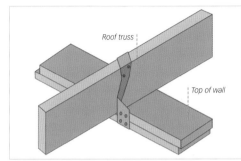

Roof truss

Top of wall

Hurricane straps keep the roof anchored to exterior walls.

- Don't forget to plan for your pets; they are not usually allowed in shelters.
- Refill any medical prescriptions required.
- Store packaged food that can be prepared without cooking, and that does not need to be kept in the refrigerator.
- Have clean, airtight containers to store several days' water supply.
- Have timber ready for protection of large windows and doors, and masking tape for use on small windows (large strips covering the glass can reduce the danger of flying glass).

- Place any important or irreplaceable documents in waterproof containers and store them in the highest possible place within your home. If you have to be evacuated, do not forget to take them with you.

Preparation is the key to surviving a hurricane.

RESPONSE AND SURVIVAL

- If staying indoors, use an inside room away from doors and windows, or an inner passageway.
- Do not venture outside in the brief calm during the passage of the eye of the storm. The lull can end suddenly as winds return from the opposite direction.
- Constantly monitor media information channels.
- If evacuation becomes necessary, leave early – in daylight if possible.
- Take survival kit basics, including: water, spare spectacles, hearing aid/batteries and personal identification.

RECOVERY

- Do not return home until official clearance has been given.
- Do not use tap water until told that it is safe to do so. Use stored water or boiled water.
- Carry out emergency repairs to prevent further damage and to safeguard your home against possible looting.
- Remember to concentrate on safety and security before comfort.
- Emergency services and insurance assessors will be very busy – be patient.

Thunderstorms and lightning

Thunderstorms can produce prodigious amounts of rain which can cause flooding, but their most terrifying component is lightning. Large hailstones may also present a danger to humans and animals.

Lightning tends to strike higher ground and objects protruding above the landscape, especially good conductors of electricity such as items

Lightning is the most dangerous element of a thunderstorm.

containing metal. Lightning may strike several miles away from the parent cloud, and almost 50 per cent of deaths and injuries caused come from currents that come up from the ground after a tall object has been struck.

It doesn't matter what you are carrying or holding, if you are the tallest object you could be the target. If severe storms are forecast, monitor weather bulletins.

If at home or work

PREPARATION

- Look for darkening skies and increased wind.
- If you hear thunder then you are close enough to be struck by lightning.
- Keep on monitoring local media for updates and warning instructions.
- Stay indoors and avoid travel if possible.
- Close windows and doors, and secure objects outside the home (e.g. patio furniture, bins, etc).
- Ensure that children and animals are inside.
- Unplug unnecessary electrical appliances (to isolate them from the mains power supply, which may conduct a power surge during a lightning storm).
- Remove rotten tree timber or any other debris that may cause a flying hazard.

RESPONSE

Avoid taking a bath or shower or running water for any purpose. This is because lightning can travel along pipes. Keep away from doors, windows, fireplaces, stoves, bathtubs, or any other electrical charge conductors. Avoid using corded phones and other electrical equipment (mobile or cordless phones are safe).

If on foot

RESPONSE

- Go to safe shelter immediately – avoid metal structures or constructions with metal sheeting.
- Ideally, find shelter in a low-lying area and make sure that the spot chosen is not likely to flood. Crouch down with feet together and head down to make yourself a smaller target.
- Hairs standing up on the back of your neck could indicate that a lightning strike is imminent.
- Do not lie flat on the ground; this will make a bigger target.
- Keep away from all utility lines (phone, power etc), metal fences, trees and hilltops.
- Do not shelter under trees as these conduct electricity.
- Rubber-soled shoes and car tyres do not offer protection from lightning.

If travelling

RESPONSE

- Get off bicycles, motorcycles or farm vehicles.
- Get to a safe shelter.
- If boating or swimming, get to land as quickly as possible and take shelter.
- During a storm remain in your vehicle until help arrives or the storm has passed (the metal roof will provide protection, if you are not touching metal inside); windows should be up; park away from trees and power lines.
- If there is a tornado involved in a storm, evacuate the vehicle and seek shelter.

TREATMENT

- IMPORTANT: If at all possible get any individual who is struck by lightning to a proper facility such as a hospital.
- See basic first aid (see pp 172–9).
- People struck by lightning carry no electric charge and can be handled safely.
- Check for broken bones, loss of hearing and eyesight.
- A victim of a lightning strike can suffer varying degrees of burning. Check the impact point and where the electricity left the body.

The distinctive rotating funnel shape of a tornado.

Tornadoes

Tornadoes, nature's most violent storms, come from powerful thunderstorms. They appear as rotating funnel-shaped clouds in which winds can top 300 mph. Tornado prediction is limited but usually there will be at least a few minutes warning. 'Tornado watch' is a period when tornadoes are possible. 'Tornado warning' is when a tornado has been sighted. That is when shelter should be taken immediately.

If at home or work
PREPARATION
- Plan your evacuation route carefully – check journey time to fixed destination.
- Fix hurricane straps to secure roof to walls (see pp 32–3).
- Ensure you know the warning signs in the weather: a dark sky, greenish in colour; wall clouds (an isolated low-hanging cloud formation beneath the rain-free portion of a thunderstorm) or large hailstones; or an approaching cloud of debris (which sounds like an advancing train).
- If such signs are evident, check the media for more information.

RESPONSE

- Shelter away from windows and doors – preferably in a basement or inner room without windows (maybe even a cupboard).
- Shelter under heavy furniture – away from falling debris and objects.
- Protect head and neck with arms.

If in a vehicle
RESPONSE

Most importantly, take shelter when a tornado is nearby. A car is the *least* safe place to be – they can be easily tossed. If a tornado is imminent and there are no strong buildings for shelter, lie flat in a ditch or other ground depression and place your arms over your head. If you do need to take refuge in a ditch, check that there isn't any flooding. If flooding starts, be ready to move quickly.

If on foot
RESPONSE

- Try to get indoors as quickly as possible.
- Never try to outrun a tornado.
- Move away from the tornado at right angles so that you are not in its path.
- If escape is not possible, shelter in a ditch or ground depression.

Avalanches

An avalanche is a mass fall of debris down a mountainside – it is usually snow, but can include rock and ice. Since avalanches are extremely unpredictable it is essential for all users of winter sport areas to be fully 'information-aware' as knowledge is the key to survival.

An avalanche seen and survived in the Alps!

Avalanches occur when the force of gravity on the snow pack, plus pressure of human presence, exceeds the friction holding snow to the slope. As gravity is a constant, the variables are the amount of snow and the amount of friction. Inadequate friction is the reason why slopes so often slide in layers, where a new fall of snow does not bind enough to the older snow beneath.

Suffocation is the greatest danger for anyone swept away by an avalanche and buried by the snow, which can compress a victim and literally squeeze the life out of them.

Time is the crucial factor in survival. From the moment someone is buried they have a 90 per cent chance of survival if rescued inside 15 minutes. Beyond half an hour the chance of survival drops to 50 per cent and that percentage decreases the longer someone remains under the snow. If a victim is more than 1.8 m (6 ft) down, survival is unlikely. Commercially available digital transceivers are a vital piece of equipment to trace people.

Nearly 95 per cent of avalanche incidents could be avoided with a greater degree of awareness. Avoiding accidents, through knowledge and correct decision-making, comes from information and preparation. That same process can drastically increase survival chances.

PREPARATION

All major ski areas post daily avalanche warnings based on local knowledge. Check the forecast before setting out and be aware of avalanche signs. If you have any doubts, do not go.

AVALANCHE SIGNS

- Steep slopes – between 25 and 45 degrees.
- Convex slopes (spoon-shaped) are the most dangerous, especially between late December and the end of January.
- North-facing slopes are most likely to see avalanches in mid-winter. South-facing slopes are also susceptible in warmer temperatures on sunny, spring days.
- Smooth, grassy slopes are more dangerous than areas bearing rocks, trees and heavy foliage, where snow has something to grip.
- New snow is the most dangerous.
- Rapid snow settlement is a good sign – loose, dry snow slides more easily.
- Loose, underlying snow is more dangerous than when compacted. Use a ski-stick to check.
- Low temperatures increase the duration of snow instability, while a sudden temperature increase can cause wet-snow slides.

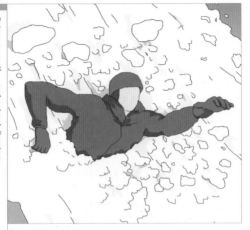

Use swimming strokes to keep on top of the snow.

RESPONSE
Try to avoid the snow slide. As a last resort, try leaping upwards as the slope breaks away.

SURVIVAL
If caught in an avalanche:
- Try to stay on the surface – you will have three times more chance of survival (see above).

- Discard all equipment.
- Seek shelter/protection – rocks or trees, for example – and hold tight.
- If you have found shelter, crouch low, in a ball, facing away from the snow slide.
- Cover nose and mouth – using a scarf helps to avoid suffocation.
- Arch hands over face to create an air space.
- Jerk arms towards surface – this can act as a marker for rescuers.
- Once the avalanche stops, begin digging out – delay can allow snow to settle.
- Try to keep calm.

If you are a survivor
- Mark the location where other team members were last seen – use clothing, a pole, anything.
- Start searching immediately below the last seen location.
- Only leave for help if you think that you can return in time – a judgement call.

If caught in a vehicle
- Switch off the engine.
- Do not smoke or use a lighter/matches – this consumes oxygen.
- If available, leave two-way radio on.

Earthquakes

Earthquakes are caused by the movement, along fault lines, in the Earth's crust, resulting in shaking, rolling and sudden ground movement. Earthquakes cannot be predicted (despite modern science working towards that), and so preparation is limited. Certain areas of the world are earthquake zones where a heightened state of preparedness is usual – such as earthquake-proof criteria for new buildings. Aftershocks are usually smaller but also dangerous because they can bring down anything weakened by the initial quake.

If at home or work

PREPARATION

- Draw curtains across windows to restrict potential shattered glass.
- Bolt or screw cupboards and bookcases to walls (a DIY manual will show you how), and keep heavy objects on lower shelves.

RESPONSE

Drop and cover:

- Drop to the floor and get under something for cover – e.g. a desk or table.

- Stay away from glass, windows or anything that can fall.
- Do not rush for doors if in a crowded place.
- Do not get into an elevator during an earthquake.
- If you smell gas or hear a hissing or blowing sound it may be a leak. Open windows – this prevents a build-up in an enclosed space.

If on foot

- Be wary of broken glass or other sharp debris on the ground, inside and outside.
- Move away from buildings, streetlights and utility structures such as telegraph poles or power lines.

If in a vehicle

- Halt vehicle as soon as safe to so do.
- Remain in vehicle until shaking stops.
- Car suspension will make the vehicle shake violently during the earthquake – but a car is still a safe place to be.
- Avoid stopping near or under buildings, overpasses or utility wires.
- When the earthquake stops, proceed with caution – avoid bridges/structures that may have been damaged.
- Be aware that aftershocks are certain.

Floods

People in the tropics have always lived with the fear of flooding, but in recent times the threat of 'nature's sledgehammer' has been an ever-increasing feature of weather in other parts of the globe. Flash floods can occur as a result of greater than normal levels of rainfall, snow melting causing rivers to overflow, or ocean waves coming ashore. Floods can vary from a few centimetres to several metres and are the greatest taker of human life in nature, killing some 1.5 million people a year.

Houses close to water need to be protected by a flood wall.

Just 15 cm (6 in) of water can knock a person off their feet, 0.5 m (1.64 ft) can sweep a car away and a depth of 3 m (9.84 ft) can demolish a building.

Floods can develop slowly, even over a period of several days, but flash floods can strike in a matter of minutes. People living in low-lying areas need to be aware of the flood plan for their area. A crucial decision – evacuate or stay put – must, if at all possible, be based on official recommendations by the authorities.

Use sandbags to limit water damage to buildings.

PREPARATION

If you build on or already live on a flood plain:

- It's advisable to get your home evaluated by a professional structural engineer.
- Install electric sockets and meters above the highest watermark of previous flooding.
- Raise boilers, fires and any fixed electrical points to a reasonable level – again, check previous watermark height.
- Fit water-resistant material as flooring – i.e. tiles rather than wood, especially to lower floor levels.
- Waterproof cellar/basement walls.
- Ensure that you have the correct insurance policy in place.

RESPONSE

If flooding is likely in your area:

- Monitor media information channels for any information on the flood.
- Ensure that you are familiar with local emergency procedures, especially assembly points and routes to those points.
- If flash flooding is likely to occur, evacuate to higher ground.
- Be aware of all likely channels that are prone to flash flooding: such as streams, rivers, drainage ditches.

IF EVACUATION IS NECESSARY

- Secure your home and collect all essential documents – for example, insurance policies, personal identification.
- Turn off the gas and electricity at the mains.
- Disconnect electrical appliances but do not touch them if they are wet or standing in water.
- Do not drive into a flooded area.
- If rising water envelops your vehicle, abandon it and seek higher ground.
- Just a few centimetres of water will reach the bottom of most cars and compromise control and engine function (cause stalling).

If moving on foot

- Do not walk through moving water unless you have to. If you have to, use a stick (or something similar) to check that the water depth in front of you is less than knee-height; if deeper, avoid, as water can hide dangers.
- Avoid power lines that have come down because of the danger of electrocution.

RECOVERY AND CLEAR-UP

- Monitor the media for information on when it is safe to return home, places to be avoided, etc.

- Some roads may still present a danger from floodwater and debris. If your path is blocked by official barriers, seek an alternate route.
- If you need to move in areas subjected to flooding, stay on firm ground as water may be charged with electricity from damaged power lines.
- Avoid walking through flood debris – there may be hidden dangers.

BACK HOME
- Ensure that your home is dry before switching the electricity supply back on.
- Do not smoke or use a naked flame in or near your home unless you are certain that there is no gas leak or flammable materials present.
- Check the integrity of all wiring, sockets and light switches. Do not use them until they have been checked by a qualified electrician if in doubt.
- Water and sewage pipes may be damaged, so they will need to be checked before you turn the water supply back on. Consult your local authority before using any water, as contamination may have occurred. (Adequate means of water purification will provide a short term measure.)
- Before cleaning up, photograph any damage for insurance purposes.

Wildfires can spread quickly and cause immense damage.

Wildfires

Wildfires on brush, or on recreational facilities such as campsites, are a real danger to humans, animals and the environment. Extreme heat and drought create ideal conditions for a wildfire to break out. Preparation can drastically reduce damage and threat to life.

If at home or work
PREPARATION
Before a wildfire approaches your home or place of work:

- Evacuate all family members (and pets) – prioritise anyone restricted by medical or physical conditions.
- Wear protective clothing, preferably fireproof or fire-resistant.
- Remove any combustible material from the immediate environment of the house to beyond the defensible area; cut down bushes and hedges that could fuel fire and be a bridge to the house.
- Clear all gulleys and roof spaces of leaves.
- Damp down house roof, walls and any trees and foliage adjacent to house which cannot be moved.

- Close and protect all openings such as vents, eaves, cellar/basement doors and windows.
- Close shutters, blinds or any non-combustible window coverings to reduce radiant heat.
- Close inside doors to reduce/prevent draft.
- Turn off the gas supply to house.
- If the fuel supply is contained in an external tank, for example, propane gas, turn off at source.
- Fill pools, ponds or any other large containers with water – useful for emergency dowsing.
- Ensure water pumps (powered by petrol) are fully fuelled.
- Take the car out of the garage, park a safe distance away, and wind up windows.
- Close the garage doors. Disconnect any automatic openers to enable hand opening.
- Place any vital or irreplaceable documents in a fireproof container, and keep them handy as rapid evacuation may be required.

RESPONSE

If evacuation is ordered by the authorities:

- Switch on outside lights and leave a light on in every room – heavy smoke will restrict visibility.
- Close but don't lock doors on departure; if you lock them and fire crews need access, they may have to force entry to fight fire.

- Keep the radio on for official announcements – you don't want to evacuate in the direction of the fire or its offshoots.

If you are trapped at home
- Stay calm. As the fire front approaches, retreat inside the house.
- Survival is possible inside. It is probable that the fire will pass before the house burns down.
- If a closed door is hot to the touch do not open – there is probably fire on the other side.

RECOVERY

After a wildfire has passed:

- Check roof immediately.
- Check house structure for any damage.
- Extinguish any burning material, sparks, or embers, and double check again later – hidden smoke, sparks and embers could re-ignite.
- Check inside the attic space for burning sparks or embers.
- Water saved in containers will be a useful resource at this stage.

IF YOU ARE CAUGHT IN THE OPEN

- The best temporary shelter is where there is little or no fuel to feed the fire; the back of a steep terrain is best, but avoid gulleys and natural chimneys.
- If there is a road close by, lie face down in the ditch alongside or on the uphill side of a ditch.
- If caught in woods, seek a ground depression in an area where there is sparse fuel for fire; clear any fuel away and lie face down until the fire passes.
- Look for pools, ponds or somewhere to take refuge until the fire passes. Do not take refuge in a fast river or stream.

If you are caught in a vehicle

RESPONSE

Only carry out the following in an emergency:

- It is possible to survive a wildfire if you stay in your vehicle. It is less dangerous than trying to outrun a fire on foot.
- Close windows and air vents.
- Drive slowly with headlights full on.
- Watch carefully for other vehicles and people on foot.
- Do not drive through heavy smoke – if you can't see what's ahead, don't risk danger.
- If you must stop, park as far as possible from trees and thickets; keep lights on and the engine off.
- Stay on the floor of your vehicle and cover your body with anything non-flammable.
- Remain in your vehicle until the fire passes, but do not run the engine (it may stall and not restart).
- Smoke and sparks may enter the vehicle. Do not panic – fuel tanks rarely explode.

RECOVERY

If you stay in your car until the fire passes:

- Check the car for any damage.
- Extinguish any burning material, sparks or embers, before restarting the car.

Tsunamis

Tsunamis occur when an ocean floor earthquake sends a mass of water radiating outwards. A tsunami or 'killer wave' can travel across the open ocean at over 600 mph and when the tidal wave hits shallow water, near the coast, the height of that wave can rise rapidly, sweeping away everything in its path. It is particularly devastating in areas around sea level.

The first wave is not always the most dangerous. Very often, secondary waves can be larger, can arrive just moments after the first wave has struck, and continue for several hours.

If a tsunami originates hundreds of miles away from landfall there is often time for the authorities to issue a warning. However, if the quake causing the tidal wave happens close to shore there may only be a few minutes to evacuate.

Tsunamis cannot be prevented but forewarning can be improved with research, and that can translate into greater advance warning to enable people to clear threatened areas.

The Pacific Rim is the most seismologically active area of the planet and is where most tsunamis occur, so populations around that area should be aware of emergency procedures. Most vulnerable are coastal regions less than 7.7 m (25 ft) above sea level and within a mile of the shoreline.

PREPARATION
- Ensure that you are familiar with the disaster survival plan (your own and official directives).
- If you feel the ground shake after becoming aware an earthquake has occurred, make for high ground immediately.
- Try for higher ground that is a minimum of

15.4 m (50 ft) above sea level and as far inland as possible – the further inland the safer.
- There are no warning signs – suddenly the ocean just appears. However, a change in the sea level at the coast (check markers such as rocks and usual water lines) is indicative that something isn't right.
- Avoid complacency. In the United States more people have died from tsunamis since 1945 than from earthquakes.

RESPONSE
- Don't be tempted to watch a tidal wave. (In Hawaii, in 1960, the wave was an hour later than predicted, and consequently caught sightseers without warning.)
- Save yourself and your family – don't try to save possessions.
- Await official clearance before returning to any evacuated area; more powerful secondary waves are likely.
- Avoid water-borne debris – it poses a hazard to people and boats.

RECOVERY
The primary concern in recovery is community restoration through:

- Shelter
- First aid and medicine.
- Water – for drinking and sanitation.
- Disease prevention.

Due to the vast scale of tsunami destruction, large-scale recovery will be dependent upon state and international aid. Remember, the infrastructure of transport and communications, essential for aid distribution, will be fragmented, at best, and non-existent at worse.

A tsunami can sweep away everything in its path.

A volcanic eruption can devastate vast areas of land.

Volcanoes

A volcano is a mountain or hill, typically conical, which has a vent running up through its centre to a crater at the top (side vents are also possible). It is through the vent that magma (molten rock) is forced, by built-up gasses deep below the earth's crust, resulting in a volcanic eruption. Such an eruption causes lava flow, which can devastate large areas of land and spew thousands of tons of rock, poisonous gasses and volcanic ash over many thousands of square miles. An understanding of what a volcano is and can do is crucial towards surviving an eruption.

Volcanoes may give advance warnings before erupting, but they can also erupt in a short space of time – a few hours or days. Although in some cases these signs can occur for years, you should pay attention to the following: rumblings from the volcano or the ground; ash and gases appearing from the top, the sides or around the volcano. Gases can kill vegetation in the area. Other signs are earth movement, whether faint tremors or earthquakes; pumice dust in the air and acid rain fall. Steam in clouds over the volcano and rotten egg smells near rivers are other indicators.

Lava flow.

A volcanic eruption can affect large areas. You should be aware that earthquakes (see pp 48–50), flash floods (see pp 51–4) and wildfires (see pp 57–61) are all life-threatening dangers that may occur far beyond the area of lava flow itself.

PREPARATION
- Learn about your community warning systems.
- If you are visiting the site of a volcano, make sure that you prepare for your trip. Learn about local issues and warnings of possible non-volcanic dangers (see above).

- If an evacuation is ordered, follow instructions from the authorities. Ensure that you know what those instructions are, especially if you are in the path of lava flow or mud flow.
- Ensure that a disaster plan is in place. Make sure all family members are familiar with the plan.
- A pair of goggles and a disposable breathing mask should be part of your disaster supply kit (for each family member).
- Don't take chances, stay away from active sites.
- Instruct each person where to meet if separated.

RESPONSE
- Bring all animals inside and put any machinery in a garage or indoors.
- If an eruption occurs in your area, evacuate immediately to avoid flying debris, gases, lateral blast and lava flow.
- Beware of mud flows – avoid stream channels and ditches, as the danger from them increases with prolonged heavy rain.
- Mud flows can move faster than you can walk or run; look upstream before crossing a bridge, and do not cross a bridge if mud flow is approaching.
- Avoid river valleys and low-lying areas.
- If you are caught outdoors when an eruption occurs, try to find shelter indoors.

PROTECTION FROM FALLING ASH

- Wear long-sleeved shirts and long trousers.
- Use eyeglasses and goggles instead of contact lenses.
- Use a dust mask or damp cloth over your face to assist breathing.
- Avoid areas downwind from the eruption to keep away from volcanic ash.
- Stay indoors until the ash has settled, unless the roof is in danger of collapsing.
- Close all doors, windows and ventilation outlets.
- Clear ash from flat or low-pitched roofs.
- Avoid running vehicle engines; driving can stir up ash and clog engines.
- Avoid driving in heavy ashfall unless absolutely necessary – keep the speed down to around 30 mph.
- Restricted areas are dangerous and must be avoided, even if lava flow is not in that area.

2

Man-made
disasters

Air crashes

Air travel, per capita, is still the safest form of transport. Between 1986 and 2005 the number of fatalities, per 100,000 hours of flying time, averaged less than two per annum. For example, in 1995 there were 867 fatalities for nearly 25 million hours travelled. Whatever the statistics illustrate, being involved in an air crash remains perhaps the most traumatic event that a human can experience. What is clear, from the investigations that follow such incidents, is that travellers can improve their chances of survival by preparation.

The passage of an air crash can be divided into four phases: Preparation, Ditching, Exiting, and Survival. There will be some obvious differences, depending on whether the aircraft goes down on land or into water.

Essential: air passengers must digest all information imparted by the cabin crew during the pre-flight briefing. It probably won't be needed, but it might save your life.

PHASE 1: PREPARATION

- Remind yourself of the pre-flight briefing by reading the plastic information card in the seat pocket.
- The aisle seats in the rear half of the plane are statistically those with the highest survival rates.
- The best seat is next to the window in an emergency exit row.
- When you board the plane, count the rows from your seat to the nearest emergency exit – in front and behind.
- Practise opening and closing the seat belt (there are several types in use today); an emergency is not the time for fumbling.
- If you are in a light/private aircraft, a life preserver should always be worn if flying over extensive water.

PHASE 2: DITCHING

- The cabin crew are your first point of reference.
- Try to remain calm.
- Remove spectacles and secure them safely about your person (a sleeve or pocket), as they could potentially shatter and break your nose.

Brace yourself correctly for impact. It's important to get your upper torso down as much as possible.

- Tighten your seat belt.
- If you do not have a seat in front of you, bend forwards with your head down, and hug your knees (see above opposite).
- If there is a seat to brace against, use it to cradle your head (see below opposite).
- If the plane ditches into water, be ready for two jolts – firstly, when the plane hits, secondly, when the nose hits the water again.
- If in a light plane that is ditching, open the door and wedge something into it to prevent it closing and possibly jamming shut on impact.

PHASE 3: EXITING THE AIRCRAFT

If a crash is forewarned, the chances of fire are lessened by the pilots ditching excess fuel.

- If you see flames outside an emergency exit, do not open.

Two versions of the brace position.

Today the majority of plane crashes have survivors.

- Only release your seat belt when ready to leave.
- White floor lights will lead to red exit row lights.
- Once on the ground, exit the aircraft quickly using emergency chutes if deployed.
- The majority of crash survivors are able to get out of the plane under their own power or with help from someone on the plane.
- Do not count on the emergency services personnel for exit help – they are unlikely to enter the plane to get you out.
- Stay low while exiting if the plane is on fire.

Exiting an aircraft that has ditched in water
- Whatever the crash conditions, exiting the aircraft swiftly is vital.
- Put on your life preserver as soon as possible.

- If the plane is floating, it is likely to sink without warning. Never re-enter.
- Take two or three deep breaths before exiting.
- Move clear of the plane to a safe distance – beware of suction before the plane sinks.
- If the plane is under water, when clear, head for the surface with your hands extended to deflect debris.

PHASE 4: SURVIVAL

If the plane has ditched into water:

- Strike for land if possible.
- Form a floating group with fellow passengers.
- Cling to anything that floats.

If the crash occurs at an airfield:

- Clear the crash scene as soon as possible.
- Emergency services should be on hand – head for them.

If the plane ditches in desert or snow:

- Stay with the plane.
- Mark out SOS with anything dark.
- Seek out any shiny surface for signalling.
- Stay cool/warm depending on the prevailing crash-site conditions.
- Prepare a fire for heat and signalling at night.

Blackouts and power cuts

Blackouts, power cuts, or power 'outages' – essentially the loss of the electricity supply to an area – are usually unpredictable, except in extreme weather situations. However, there are a number of contingencies that can be put into place to lessen the impact of a power shortage.

Items that need to be easily accessible in an emergency.

PREPARATION
- If you have a fireplace/stove, keep a good supply of wood.
- If you are using a generator, keep the fuel supply in secure containers.
- Avoid lifts/elevators if a blackout is predicted.
- Ensure that you have two or three days' worth of food supplies.
- If there is space available in the fridge/freezer, consider filling plastic containers with water (leaving a few centimetres/an inch for expansion). This chilled/frozen water will help keep food cold for several hours.
- Consider purchasing a non-electric heater.

RESPONSE
- Don't leave your home or workplace during a blackout unless absolutely necessary.
- Disconnect any appliances that were in use when the power went out; a power surge on restoration can cause damage.
- Leave one light on – this will indicate when the power has been restored.
- Make sure that the fridge/freezer door is closed – it will keep food fresher for longer.
- If you must eat food that was refrigerated or frozen, check carefully for signs of spoilage.

- Use the telephone in an emergency only.
- Listen to a portable radio for information updates.
- Only use a torch/flashlight in an emergency (to conserve the batteries).
- If necessary use candles, but be aware that they are a potential fire hazard, and burn oxygen.
- Never run a generator inside the home.
- When using a generator, connect the equipment to be used directly to the generator outlets. Do not connect the generator to the home electrical system.

SURVIVAL
- If the weather is hot, move to the lowest level inside your home, as cool air falls.
- If the weather is cold, wear layers of thin clothing rather than one layer of thick clothing.
- Drink plenty of water, even if you are not thirsty (to avoid dehydration).

RECOVERY
To avoid power surges on the resumption of power:
- Shift electricity usage to non-peak times.
- Avoid using non-essential electrical appliances and equipment.
- Unplug all appliances when not in use.
- Turn off radiators in unused rooms.

Fire

All buildings, whether domestic or business, should have adequate preparation in place in the event of a fire – from emergency evacuation procedures to strategically placed alarms and fire extinguishers. All persons should be familiar with emergency plans, and exit routes should be clearly defined. Drills for employees (or, if at home, a 'walk through') practising what to do in the event of an incident should take place regularly.

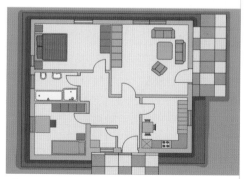

A floor plan makes it easy to see your exit route.

Locate smoke alarms at the top and bottom of stairs.

PREPARATION

Your local fire department should be happy to advise you on fire-prevention measures.

- Smoke alarms should be fitted in all buildings. Properly functioning alarms can improve the chances of surviving a fire by 50 per cent.
- The smoke alarms should be located on every level of a building. They should be positioned outside bedrooms (high on the wall or on the ceiling), and at the top and bottom of the stairs.
- Test the alarms at least monthly.
- Replace batteries regularly – testing will show if it is necessary to replace them more than annually.
- Try to ensure that there are at least two escape routes from every room.
- Note possible escape aids, such as trees, balconies or adjoining roofs.
- Ensure that your windows will open – test them regularly and check for ease of opening (from the inside).
- Consider having escape ladders, collapsible or rope ones, if your residence consists of more than one level.
- Do not accumulate old newspapers or combustible material. Do not store flammable liquids in the house. Do not smoke or have naked flame near combustible material.

- Discard any material that may have been used to wipe up flammable liquids, e.g. brush cleaners.
- Ensure that all heating appliances are maintained regularly by qualified personnel.
- Always keep matches and lighters locked away from children.
- Do not run electric wire/cord under carpets or in areas of heavy foot traffic.
- Keep fire extinguishers at strategic points, and ensure functionality; it is important that everyone knows how to use them.

RESPONSE
- Exit immediately, if possible.
- If you are trapped by fire, stay close to the floor – heat and smoke rises.

If your clothing catches fire:
- A shower will douse the fire quickly.
- Do not run – rushing air will only accelerate the burning.
- Drop to the ground and roll to extinguish flames.

ESCAPING A FIRE
- Before opening a door, check it for heat.
- Use the back of your hand to test the temperature at the top of door, the knob and the frame before opening. If hot, do not open. Do not use the palms or fingers because, if the door is hot, you will suffer burns.
- If you are unable to escape through a door, use a window.
- If it is too high to jump from a window, tie sheets together to form a ladder.
- If no escape is possible, try to attract attention by waving something.
- If smoke permeates your location, stay on the floor.
- If you can leave the room, close the door behind you – this will slow down the progress of the fire. Crawl low.
- Do not go back for your possessions.
- Once clear of the fire, call emergency services.

Gas leaks and explosions

Unlike some explosions, the time lapse between awareness and detection of a gas leak and it leading to an explosion can allow for evacuation – which may minimise or eliminate casualties. Even before a gas leak it is worth having certain preparations in place, based on S.E.C: Shut off, Evacuate and Call.

If possible, the gas supply should be shut off at source. The building and immediate area should be evacuated quickly, and from a safe place the emergency services should be contacted.

PREPARATION

All homes and workplaces should have an emergency procedure in place and at least two escape routes for each room, if possible. A floor plan for each floor should be familiar to all occupants.

- Floor plan diagrams should be strategically placed in each room, especially children's rooms.
- All family members/employees should know how to shut off the gas supply.

Natural gas has a distinct, noxious smell. If such a smell is detected:

- Open windows.
- Check the pilot light to see if it is ignited.
- If the pilot light is out, wait for the odour to dissipate before re-igniting.

RESPONSE

If you cannot locate the source of a leak or you hear a hissing sound:

- Evacuate.
- Move well clear of windows and other potential debris hazards.
- Do not use lighters.
- Do not turn light switches on or off.
- Call the emergency services.

Everyone at home should know how to turn off the gas supply.

SURVIVAL

If it has been possible to call the emergency services, they will not take long to respond. Remind yourself and any other survivors of this. If you have evacuated the building, you may need to inform rescue personnel of details of the leak and explosion that may assist them – for example, how many people were in the building at the time.

IF YOU HAVE TO STAY WHERE YOU ARE

If an explosion occurs and you cannot exit the immediate area:

- Dive for cover under a sturdy table or desk.
- Once the debris has finished falling, exit the area if possible – subsequent explosions may follow.
- If you are trapped under debris, try to keep calm.
- If you are alone, talk to yourself or do mental agility exercises.
- If you are trapped with others, talk to each other to maintain calmness.
- Try to signal your location with a torch.
- Tapping on pipes, walls or the floor may help rescuers plot your location, as could whistling.
- If the air is dusty, cover your mouth with clothing or fabric to filter breathing.
- Do not shout – open mouths risk dust inhalation.

Maritime accidents

Survival at sea is arguably the most difficult of all disaster situations. In addition, extremes of temperature can further hinder survival chances. To enhance survival, precautionary measures need rapid implementation.

Most maritime fatalities are due to a lack of preparation. Key factors in survival are adequate clothing, flotation equipment, and knowledge of survival techniques. None of those who survived the sinking of the Titanic, but failed to board lifeboats, were alive when rescue ships arrived, less than two hours later. Many would have been saved had they known how to cope in cold water, which removes body heat 25 times faster than does cold air.

The 1946 Talbot Report, into the 45,000 seamen who died during World War II, blamed the inadequacy of the Royal Navy lifebelt as a major factor.

PREPARATION

Knowledge of emergency procedures is essential. Most passenger ships are legally required to comply with SOLAS (Safety of Life at Sea) legislation. Regular lifeboat and fire drills are mandatory to familiarise passengers and crew with how to act in the event of an emergency at sea. Do not miss the drills – they may save your life. You should also be familiar with techniques to help you survive in the water (see page 91).

RESPONSE

Abandon ship only if necessary – even an incapacitated ship offers better protection than open water. Response will depend on whether a life raft is available or a survivor has to float. Before leaving the ship, consider all aspects such as fire, explosion or sinking. Consider also the environment that you are entering; weigh up the pros and cons of safety before deciding.

An incapacitated ship can offer better protection than water.

LIFE RAFTS

- Launch only when it is safe to do so (when free from obstruction or people).
- Wait until the raft is inflated before boarding it.
- Board directly onto the raft if possible – avoid or minimise the time spent in the water.
- If you must enter the water, do so gradually.
- Deploy the sea anchor.
- Secure the entrance to conserve heat.
- Take seasickness medication.
- Appoint a lookout at the entrance.
- The life raft should remain close to where the ship went down – if it is safe to do so.
- Wear as many layers of clothing as possible (obviously dependent on time factor when abandoning ship).

SURVIVAL IN THE WATER

Without the extra security of a life raft, being in the water becomes a self-preservation situation.

- First priority: remain calm. Panicking is counter-productive (it also consumes precious energy); fear hastens exhaustion.
- A broken limb can still function if splinted.

- Do not swim unless necessary – your energy might be needed later.
- If you don't get a life preserver, grab anything you can for buoyancy.
- Floating is the easiest way of conserving energy in the water.
- Try to float (on your back) with your legs together, elbows at your side and arms across your chest – this reduces body heat loss.
- If you have left the area to clear the sinking ship, returning to the scene may procure floating debris for buoyancy.
- Water and fuel containers aid flotation.
- Use clothing as floats. Inflate clothing by removing, securing ends of sleeves and trousers and sweeping through the air – the trapped air can buy vital minutes before re-inflating becomes necessary (see opposite).
- Big breaths that fill the lungs, help flotation.
- If injury prevents you floating on your back, float face down, raising your head periodically to take in air.
- If there is fuel burning on the water, swim underwater to clear the danger area.
- Before surfacing, put one arm clear of the surface and clear a safe area before emerging to breathe.

Use clothing as floats – trousers work well.

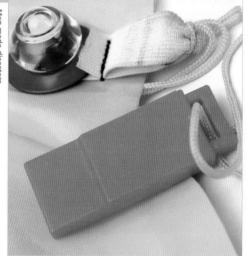

Always carry life jackets if you are out on boats or sailing.

- Have a signalling device – such as a whistle, mirror or lighter – in your pocket.
- Strike for shore if safe and close enough – if you can't see shore, floating twigs or vegetation can indicate the proximity of land.

Avoiding hypothermia or extreme heat

If you are cold:

- The more layers of clothes you are able to don, the better your chances are of slowing down the loss of body heat. Even wet clothing can do this, particularly woollen garments.
- Difficult though it may be to do, you may have to take clothes from dead bodies if you haven't enough clothing yourself.
- Exercise will not warm you – it merely accelerates the loss of body heat.

In extreme heat it is crucial to protect the head, eyes and skin from the sun:

- Swimming or wetting clothing can cool the body.
- Saltwater removes the skin's natural moisture while sunburn accelerates dehydration – protect the skin with light clothing.

THE NEXT STAGE OF SURVIVAL

The next stage in survival concerns food and water, especially if a long period before rescue is likely.

Water

- Despite a common belief that drinking seawater is not good for humans, it may save your life. French scientist Dr Alain Bombard survived for nine weeks whilst crossing the Atlantic in 1952 on nothing other than what the sea provided – water and food.

- In large doses, drinking salt water can cause kidney damage and accelerate dehydration, but in small doses it can work. We are talking *survival* here, not health.
- Rainwater can be trapped using anything available such as sheeting or waterproof material. Be prepared for rain collection – if you wait until it rains you may be too late.

Food

- The oceans are full of fish – makeshift tackle (see below) such as bent safety pins at the end of string or wool can extend survival periods.
- Birds can be caught but fish are easier to catch.

Makeshift fishing tackle: safety pin, thorn(s), wood and nail.

Rail crashes

Millions of passengers travel the world's rail network blissfully unaware that in the event of a crash their chances of survival are dependent upon two factors: information and preparation.

Maintenance and repair of the rail infrastructure is the responsibility of the operators, as is providing information to the public for their health and safety. For their part, passengers need to assimilate this information and prepare for the unexpected.

The age of the rolling stock is also a consideration when a crash occurs, as the adequacy of safety measures will have a crucial bearing on crash survivors exiting carriages.

In the event of a train crash, the first point of reference should be the rail staff, but if they are incapacitated it falls upon the individual to know what course of action to take. Because of the diversity of rolling stock, throughout the world, generalising about safety can be problematic. However, certain steps can be applied.

PREPARATION

- Ensure that your mobile/cell phone is fully charged and functional before travelling.

- Check emergency procedure information before beginning your journey – if possible, obtain it before boarding, as information may not be available on the train.
- Note the location of emergency exits, the first aid box and fire extinguishers.
- Stow luggage securely. Flying cases present two dangers: they could become flying missiles or could hinder your exit from the crashed vehicle.
- Some trains have floor-to-ceiling posts and divisions that become barriers when a carriage is on its side – note their position in relation to your seat before your journey starts.
- Be aware of the procedures to follow if an emergency evacuation becomes necessary.

RESPONSE

In the event of a crash, if possible, instructions from staff should be followed. Failing that, the following could save your life if immediate danger is present:

- Of prime concern is personal safety.
- Assess the situation as far as personal injury is concerned.
- Assess if further danger is likely (fire or smoke). If safe to do so, wait in the train until instructed otherwise.
- A smoke-filled carriage can double your exit time.

Divisions can block your exit if the train overturns.

Move away from the track after evacuation.

- Try to keep calm – emergency services should be quickly on site.

Exiting a carriage

Many carriages will have three exit options. In order of priority and safety they are:

- Exit to next carriage.
- Exterior doors – most doors have a release lever adjacent; if not, open the door using the exterior handle.
- Emergency window.

If you need to exit via an emergency window:

- Find the tool – usually in a small glass cabinet – to break the window.
- Strike the window – possibly in the corner– repeatedly, until the panes break.
- Create an exit in the window – using a piece of luggage will be safer than risking injury.

RECOVERY

- If evacuation has been necessary, leave the immediate site and move a safe distance away.
- If the emergency services are on the scene, head towards them.
- If clear of the crash and there is no sign of the emergency services, wait and try to keep calm.

Mass riots and civil unrest

Although there is a clear distinction between mass civil disorder in your own country and overseas there are certain common factors applicable to both in terms of what to do if caught up in such a situation. The main advice is obvious: avoid, if at all possible.

Take government advice before travelling to areas of conflict.

Overseas

It is important to be aware of the stability of any overseas region that you are planning to travel to. Government offices and the appropriate embassy are essential sources of information. (Check their websites or telephone them.) Adhere to the advice given and, if there is instability in that region, only travel if necessary.

PREPARATION

- Cultural and language differences can be potentially crucial; learn as much as possible before travelling.
- Before you depart, leave a clear travel itinerary with appropriate contact details: phone, mobile, e-mail address, etc.
- Ensure that you carry relevant contact details: home, friends, embassy, etc.
- Secure your passport in a safe place, and make a copy.
- Check that your affairs are in order: will, deeds of ownership, all legal documents, etc.
- If intending to drive, obtain an international driving licence.

RESPONSE

If you are caught up in a riot or civil disorder, use

common sense. Trust your instincts and avoid trouble if at all possible.

- If you are outside, stay calm – for your own welfare and to avoid attracting attention.
- Avoid confrontation – steer clear of any potential trouble.
- Be careful about what you wear – avoid quasi-military attire.
- If you are swept along in a crowd, the key is self-preservation. Keep away from walls and pillars (barriers of any type that could crush). Keep your hands free and loosen any tie (scarves should be removed). Get free of the crowd as soon as possible.
- If inside, remain indoors, away from windows.
- If you are in a hotel, ensure that you know all the exit locations.
- Know where the hotel fire alarms are located – this could make a useful diversionary tactic.
- If you assess that the situation is out of control, make plans to leave the country immediately (a pre-planned route is desirable).
- Leave the building through safest exit (windows may be more appropriate than doors).
- Evacuate as a group, especially if traversing wide-open areas is necessary – multiple targets are less obvious than individual figures.

- Walk – don't run, unless your life is under immediate threat. The human eye spots someone running quicker than at pedestrian rate; running may generate excitement that attracts a pursuer.
- If you need to take a taxi, use a licensed one.

In a car
- Check your fuel before departing.
- Do not stop for anything – a car is a useful weapon, even against a mob.

- If you can't drive forwards, use reverse.
- Drive on backstreets avoiding main routes.
- Be prepared to surrender your car or valuables if necessary – if a roadblock is encountered, bartering may be essential.
- The embassy or airport must be your priority destination.

If at home

If you are at home when an incident of civil disorder occurs, the major decision to be made will be whether to stay put or leave. It will depend on risk assessment and information from the authorities.

RESPONSE
- Stay put if it is safe to do so.
- Block all doors and windows, especially on the ground floor.
- Stay as far inside the house as possible – inner rooms or hallways are best.
- Remain as a group – you don't want family members wandering, especially if the power is off.
- Monitor official news channels – police and law enforcement agencies should not be long in reaching affected areas.
- Stay calm.

3

Terrorism

Chemical or biological attacks

Preparation for terrorist attacks involving chemical or biological agents is similar to that outlined in Nuclear Attacks (see pp 118–24), but there are some important differences which are specific to the type of attack. Firstly, the fundamental difference between biological and chemical must be understood.

BIOLOGICAL AGENTS

Biological agents are organisms, found in nature, which can be altered to kill, or debilitate, people, animals and crops. There are three basic groups most likely to be used as weapons: bacteria, viruses, and toxins. Fortunately, most agents of this kind are extremely difficult to grow and maintain whilst others, such as anthrax, are very long-living. The four methods of delivering such agents are:

- Aerosols which disperse the agents into the air where they can drift for considerable distances and infect many miles from the release point.
- Animals (many species, from insects to livestock) who can be used to contaminate.
- Food and water contamination; organisms can be long-lasting in water and food, but most microbes can be destroyed by boiling/cooking.

- Person to person — the number of infectious agents that can be spread this way is mercifully small. Smallpox, plague and the Lassa viruses have been inflicted in this way.

CHEMICAL AGENTS

Chemical agents are poisonous liquids and solids possessing a toxic effect similar to that of biological ones, but they are difficult to produce. They can be delivered through the air, by spraying or via a bomb. Such agents may only take seconds to be effective or their effect may be delayed by a few hours to a couple of days. Delivery of potentially lethal agents, in large doses, is extremely difficult and in the open air these agents can dissipate very quickly.

Some chemical agents are odourless and tasteless thus increasing the difficulty of detection and reaction. The agents are most effective around dawn or sunset when air pollution is at its worst, but it's important to remember that to launch a chemical attack is hard enough to do with military personnel and equipment, imagine how hard it would be for terrorists. However, being alert will help reduce the effect of such terrorism considerably.

Chemical attacks usually occur without warning so tell-tale signs must be noted (see page 110), especially if the agents used are quick-acting.

SIGNS OF A CHEMICAL ATTACK

- Difficulty in breathing.
- Eye irritation.
- Loss of coordination.
- Nausea.
- Burning sensation in nose, throat, and lungs.
- General signs may be dead animals, insects, or dead foliage, which might indicate the release of a chemical agent.
- Excessive saliva.
- Stomach cramps.

PREPARATION

- Shelter should be readied (see page 121). Important: Unlike the response to a nuclear incident, the room designated as a shelter, ideally with water supply, should be as high in a structure as possible (to avoid vapours that sink to low levels.
- Pre-cut plastic sheets should be ready for covering doors and windows.

RESPONSE

If an evacuation is ordered, monitor media outlets, especially local agencies, for instructions in emergency procedures. All families should have their own emergency plan (see page 136), which should be rehearsed and known to all family members in case official advice is not possible. If told to evacuate, do so quickly and calmly.

If told by local authorities to remain at home
- Close all doors and windows – cover and seal gaps or drafts with duct tape or similar.
- Turn off all ventilation in the home, especially those systems which allow outside air to enter.
- Block off chimneys, fans, etc.
- Do not go outside until told it is safe to do so.

Seal any gaps around windows with duct tape.

If caught outside

- Immediately move as far away as possible, upwind, from the contaminated area.
- Do not panic – breathing faster will increase the intake of any agent.
- Seek shelter as fast as possible.
- Don't shelter in a car unless you have no choice.

Decontamination after exposure to a chemical agent.

DECONTAMINATION

If exposed to a chemical agent, decontamination is required ASAP.

- Do not pull any clothing over your head; it should be cut off instead.
- Wash thoroughly any skin area that has been in contact with the chemical with large amounts of soapy water.
- Eyes, if affected, should be rinsed in clean water for 15 minutes.
- Spectacles should also be washed.
- Dispose of any affected clothing in a black bin bag; seal and then seal inside another bag.
- Ensure that your change of clothing is uncontaminated – if from a drawer or cupboard they should be suitable.

SURVIVAL

Emergency services will be under severe pressure in the event of a bio-terrorist attack. If you survive and have prepared well you should be able to wait for outside help.

Dirty bombs

The most likely nuclear weapon that a
terrorist might employ is a radiological
dispersal device (RDD), more commonly
known as a 'dirty bomb'. This device uses a
conventional explosive, a bomb, which acts
as the delivery vehicle for radioactive material.
As this weapon uses waste material, which
is a by-product of nuclear power and is not
safeguarded as securely as conventional
nuclear weapons, it is far easier to obtain.

A 'dirty bomb' is less effective than conventional nuclear weaponry and the casualty rate from the dispersal of radioactive material from such a weapon would be much less. There would be more damage from the explosive than from the contamination it would disperse. The 'dirty bomb' is designed for psychological impact rather than physical effect, as the panic and terror created would cause widespread disruption.

As the main danger from a 'dirty bomb' is the explosion itself, anticipation of injury and property damage should be the main concern. Because of the nature of an attack of this type, preparing for it is difficult – so response and recovery are the main focus.

RESPONSE

Any group should stay together, which is applicable to whether you are outdoors or inside a building. If group members are caught in separate buildings they should stay there until told that it is safe to leave. This also applies to places of work and to schools.

If outdoors and within range of a detonation

- Cover your nose and mouth, with a cloth if possible, to reduce the risk of inhaling any radioactive material.

- Avoid contact with any debris caused by the explosion – it may be radioactive.
- Seek immediate shelter – ideally a building with windows and doors still intact.
- Once inside, remove your outer clothing and seal it in plastic shopping bags or bin bags.
- Dispose of the cloth used to protect your nose and mouth in the same way.
- Secure the bag well away from people until the authorities give notification of the next step.
- Monitor local media information outlets for official advice.
- Wash thoroughly, from head to toe, with very soapy water.

If indoors and within range of a detonation

- Stay inside if walls, windows and doors have not been compromised.
- Shut all windows, seal all openings and fill any gaps to keep radioactive dust from penetrating the building.
- If any damage has occurred to the outer fabric of your house, seek shelter as far into the centre of the structure as possible.
- If you have to leave one building that has been damaged to go to another, make sure that you cover your mouth and nose during the transfer.

- Clothes removal, disposal and ablutions, should then follow.

RECOVERY

Because it is not possible to taste, smell or feel radiation, it will be difficult to determine whether or not contamination has occurred. Emergency services will have the necessary equipment to test people and the immediate environment.

There may only be symptoms of contamination in the case of higher levels of radiation. Symptoms, should they occur in the person exposed, may include nausea, vomiting, diarrhoea, and a reddening and swelling of the skin. If any of these symptoms manifest themselves, a doctor should be consulted immediately.

Emergency services will test the environment for radiation.

Nuclear attacks

Major cities are the most likely targets for a nuclear attack. However, if you live near a potential primary target – such as a government building or military installation – you might wish to seriously consider your location if you are worried about a potential nuclear attack.

Ignore instructions from emergency services at your peril.

Much misinformation exists about non-survivability of a nuclear attack. Noting relevant and accurate information can improve your chances of survival. Shelter (see page 121), whether specific or makeshift, can be the difference between fatal exposure to radiation or a survivable dose.

The fallout of radioactive material, in the immediate post-blast period, will deposit close to ground zero. Fortunately, the initial hazard quickly loses its intensity because of the energy it emits. For example, fallout emitting gamma ray radiation, which is fatal within an hour of exposure, is only one tenth as strong less than eight hours later. Inside 48 hours, that falls to a strength of one hundredth.

The first major decision to be made is whether to stay or go. Preparation already in place, the nature of the attack and how much store you place in the information being distributed, will all affect your decision. You will have to decide if the benefit of evacuation outweighs the risks of staying put. You do not want to be caught between the two. If evacuation is necessary, don't hesitate – go quickly and take adequate supplies.

PREPARATION

- Know exactly what the warning sound, signalling an alert, for your town or city is.

- Monitor official government information channels.
- Make evacuation plans – be conversant with official emergency plans procedure.
- Determine an evacuation destination; plan and choose a suitable route and ensure that all family members know the details.
- Remember that most routes are likely to be very crowded.
- If you live near a potential primary target that is not in a major city, consider a shelter, or a room/inner section of the house, which can be used as a shelter.
- If you live in an apartment building, check with the building manager for the appropriate emergency procedure plan, especially if there's a designated shelter.
- Do not assume evacuation is certain or possible.
- If restriction to your home is likely, ensure adequate stock of basic survival supplies (see pp 180–4).
- Locate supplies in your designated shelter.
- Try to fill as many containers as possible with water (sealed ones are best). Baths, washing machines and even garbage containers, can be used as long as they have been cleaned thoroughly and a bin liner or two inserted. Plastic soft drinks bottles are ideal and are also easy to stack.

- Water and food containers should be washed to prevent contamination to contents when opened.
- Pre-cut plastic sheeting should be readied for covering doors and windows if your shelter or designated room has an exterior wall.

BUILDING A SHELTER

The main purpose of any shelter is to provide a barrier between yourself and any radiation. The denser the mass in that barrier, the more likely you are to avoid exposure to critical levels of radiation.

- Build a shelter close to where the people who will use it live, and as low as possible.
- If a basement or similar below-ground facility is unavailable, reinforcing an existing above-ground structure is a good alternative. The mass, or barrier, between the centre of a shelter and the point where fallout would settle can be increased in many ways – for example, heavy furniture, wooden doors, sandbags, and even cardboard boxes packed with earth or books.
- When building a shelter or creating one inside an existing structure, leave space for exit and entry.
- Designate a room or inner space as your shelter.
- Ensure that supplies are easily found in the dark. as power may go off.

For shelter reinforce an existing above-ground structure.

RESPONSE
Outside
If you are outside when a nuclear attack occurs:

- Hit the floor and seek cover – preferably upwind from the blast.
- Don't look at the blast – this can cause blindness.
- Find a ditch, hill or building for cover; keep low.
- Seek better shelter as soon as possible.
- Move from the blast upwind or at a 90° angle.

In a vehicle
If you are in your car when a nuclear attack occurs:

- Lower windows to avoid flying glass.
- Get as low as possible in the car.
- Shield your face and eyes at all times.

RECOVERY

Following any terrorist attack involving exposure to radioactivity certain procedures must be carried out:

- Primary concern is to assess and treat any life-threatening injuries.
- Decontaminate any open wounds to minimise the chances of radioactivity passing into the blood stream.
- Remove victims from the immediate area of exposure to a proper medical facility if possible.

Unless exposure to radiation is obvious, as in a nuclear detonation, it can be extremely difficult to ascertain if someone has been the victim of a terrorist radiological attack. Symptoms may not appear for several days or even weeks, but if any of the following symptoms occur, the victim should be taken immediately to a medical professional:

- Burn-like lesions without any heat exposure.
- Bleeding from lips or nose.
- Hair loss.
- Tiredness, general fatigue and body ache.
- Vomiting, nausea and diarrhoea.
- Ulceration.

The after-effects of radioactive fallout can last for a long time. Be prepared for a long period of recovery.

- Normal water supplies will be contaminated for some time, but water already in pipes and taps may be used if purified.
- Use water saved in open-topped containers before starting on sealed containers.
- Radiation fallout levels decrease after the initial 24 hours following a nuclear explosion but will affect soil, and water sources, for a long time.

RADIOLOGICAL ATTACK

The major differences between radiation exposure and contamination are as follows. Not everyone exposed to a radiation source becomes radioactive; contamination occurs when minute particles of radioactive material settle on any surface, skin or clothing, and internal contamination may take place if those particles:

- are ingested
- are inhaled
- enter the body via an open wound.

If contamination does take place, decontamination must be implemented without delay. However, contamination is not contagious and cannot be passed on to another human.

Plane hijacking

Of all terrorist incidents, a plane hijacking is arguably the most traumatic as it inevitably involves face-to-face contact with someone intending harm to you or others. The events of 11 September 2001 radically changed the world's perception of hijacking and what response there should be – by passengers and the authorities. Hijackings are extremely rare, however.

The guidelines detailed in this section were actually drawn up prior to the 11 September attacks and before the brave passengers of United Flight 93 ignored those guidelines and prevented the fourth plane hijacked that day from hitting its target. The sacrifice of ordinary people, who ignored official advice and tackled the hijackers, has passed into public consciousness.

The crucial factor in passengers determining their response of action is the purpose of the hijacking. If the terrorists' intention is to take hostages for political purpose or a stunt to publicise a cause then the guidelines still hold true. But if, as in the 11 September attacks, the intention is to use the aircraft as a flying bomb, passengers might have to act as those on Flight 93 did.

Troops practise how to unarm a hijacker.

RESPONSE

Calmness, however difficult, must be the prime aim. Hijackers may be just as nervous as their hostages, so nothing should be done that could antagonise them and disturb any calmness achieved.

- Encourage others to be calm.
- Avoid making any physical or verbal challenge to the hijackers.

- Think carefully before attempting escape – you must be certain of success, otherwise don't try. The hijackers who are visible may not be alone; others may remain anonymous until security personnel reveal themselves.
- If there is shooting, hit the floor and hold on tight – decompression may occur if the plane is in flight.

After the takeover phase may come the longest stage of the hijacking:
- Try to set your mind into relaxed mode – you could be there for a long time.
- Be aware that there may be physical torment from the hijackers.
- Avoid eye contact with hijackers.
- Try to keep still – this avoids drawing your captors' attention.
- Keep your mind busy – make mental notes of the hijackers (their physical appearance, mannerisms, etc.).
- If you carry both an official and a visitor's passport, hand over the latter if the hijackers demand ID.
- If addressed by a hijacker, answer calmly and without emotion – keep answers succinct. Answer factually, without opinion.

RESOLUTION

This is the final phase of any hijacking. It may be that a rescue operation is mounted. This will be a last resort and may require drastic action on the part of the passengers.

- You must keep calm.
- If shots are fired, hit the floor and stay there.
- If smoke or fire is present, head for the emergency exits, that is unless rescue forces state otherwise.
- Once clear of the plane, look for instruction from the emergency services or rescue personnel.
- If there is no-one to advise you, leave the immediate vicinity of the plane and make for the terminal or control tower.
- Rescue personnel may treat you as a hijacker in the chaos – don't make sudden movements, and obey any instructions given.
- If a fight for life becomes necessary, you might have to.

Suicide bombers

One of the simplest forms of attack, yet one of the hardest to detect: that's the consensus of opinion amongst the world's counter-terrorist agencies when it comes to suicide bombers. Whether such terrorists strap explosives to their person or fly hijacked airliners into targets, they are difficult to identify. Paradoxically, there are very few tell-tale signs to identify such terrorists because, if there were, they would alter their modus operandi.

Since the attacks of 11 September 2001, the world has been in a heightened state of awareness, and members of the public are encouraged to be vigilant and observant, and to report anything suspicious to the authorities.

Suicide bombers rarely hit randomly – targets are usually 'soft' where maximum casualties can be inflicted, such as shopping centres or recreational facilities, which involve large crowds. A lot of preparation goes into such missions, and during that stage terrorists' behaviour could give them away to a careful observer.

HAVE YOU ...

- Seen anyone recording, filming or taking notes near potential targets, such as police stations, transport termini or military installations?
- Spotted anyone asking questions about a key installation?
- Noted anyone who seems out of place in a particular environment?
- Been aware of any rehearsal or dry run that possibly involved timing traffic lights or monitoring traffic flow?
- Observed vehicles that seem to have been abandoned for no apparent reason?
- Spotted dead plants near a building that were not

dead previously? Some bomb-making equipment produces poisonous fumes that kill vegetation. The same fumes can also bleach facial hair.

It may seem exaggerated but if the answer to any of the above is yes, even if they are only suspicions, it is worth reporting it.

SPOTTING A POTENTIAL SUICIDE BOMBER
People-watching is a modern phenomenon, but, in the case of suicide bombers, behavioural irregularities may just give clues that could prevent a terrorist attack. Things that are out of the ordinary could also indicate a possible attack is imminent.

The FBI has issued, to many US law enforcement agencies, possible suicide bombers' indicators:

- Look out for anyone wearing bulky clothing when the weather obviously does not require such apparel.
- Note any chemical smells that seem to be inappropriate.
- Nervous behaviour from anyone displaying any of the above.
- Unmilitary behaviour from anyone in uniform – stolen uniforms are a favourite terrorist method for 'blending in'.
- If you have any doubts, report them.

Suspect packages

A suspect package might be anything from a letter bomb to an incendiary device, with any number of explosive variations in between. Whatever the contents, such a package should be left untouched until the proper response, namely police or armed forces experts, arrive on the scene.

Explosive and incendiary devices account for around 90 per cent of all terrorist attacks. Bombs are designed to inflict maximum casualties whilst the prime objective of incendiary devices is to cause fires.

The following information is relevant to a suspect package being found in a vehicle as well as in the home or at work.

PREPARATION
- Never accept any mail that arouses suspicion.
- Letter bombs can be as dangerous as packages.

RESPONSE
- Suspicious packages or letters should not be touched and never moved.
- Any movement of such a package, especially cutting tape or binding, could cause it to explode.

- Putting a suspect package in water could detonate it.

SIGNS OF A SUSPICIOUS PACKAGE

There are a number of indicators or signs – some more obvious than others – that *could* suggest that a letter or parcel might contain a bomb. Things to look out for:

- Unusual odour – many explosives give off smells like shoe polish or almonds.
- Oily stains on the package.
- Protruding wires, etc.
- The postmark is from an unknown location.
- Incorrect spelling, or the address poorly typed.
- The address has an incorrect title or uses only a title and no name – e.g. Mr Smith.
- Restrictive marking – e.g. 'confidential', 'strictly for personal attention of', etc.
- Excessive postage – this could indicate the sender's reluctance to have it weighed at the post office counter.
- The package has an unusual size, shape, weight, or is lopsided (weight unevenly distributed).
- The envelope is rigid or contents uneven.
- There is excessive string or binding around the package.

SURVIVAL

- If the package or letter is regarded as suspicious after delivery, leave the building and notify authorities. Make sure that no-one goes back for anything.
- If the package is left on or in a vehicle, leave immediately; be calm and alert.
- Any bystanders should move to a safe distance/location – and notify authorities.
- Don't worry if the package ultimately turns out to be someone's lunch – it may not have been.

Notify the authorities if you see a suspicious package.

Home safety

For the ordinary citizen in the 21st century, the uncertainty of a terrorist attack can be as frightening as the attack itself. However, vigilance, awareness, and common sense can help prevent and minimise such attacks as well as aid recovery.

No one, terrorists excepted, can determine their location when a terrorist incident occurs. The nature of such an attack can also vary, from bombs in London and Madrid, to hijacking planes for use as flying missiles, as in the 11 September attacks.

Generally, terrorists attack high-profile targets with the aim of causing maximum damage and casualties and achieving global media exposure. Governments have emergency procedures in place to deal with terrorist disasters, but it is often the reactions of the victims themselves that is the key to their survival.

Terrorist disasters are most likely to affect people at work or whilst travelling. However, there may be collateral damage, especially if chemical or biological materials are used, that affect people in the home.

PREPARATION

Being aware of your immediate environment will help determine anything out of the ordinary.

- Have a home emergency plan in place, including telephone numbers for the emergency services (but be aware that mobile phone networks may be overloaded). Designate a safe place well away from your home for possible evacuation, and ensure that family members know how to get there safely if separated.
- Monitor official information outlets – including websites and radio.
- Secure all windows and doors against any possible intrusion.
- All family members should have contact details for each other – mobile/cell phones, pagers, etc.
- Establish emergency exits, ensuring that they open quickly from inside.
- Secure important documents.
- Remember, safety is the prime concern and not possessions.

RESPONSE

If a terrorist disaster strikes:

- Assess the situation – decide whether to stay put or evacuate. You may need official advice. Stay where you are if there is no immediate danger.
- Check for injuries – yourself and others – and administer first aid if necessary.
- Check for damage to your home (using a torch).

Emergency procedures include cordoning-off affected areas.

- Check for gas leaks – turn off mains.
- Shut down electricity and water if told to do so by the authorities.
- Let a designated contact know that you are okay.
- Check on neighbours, especially if vulnerable.
- Be aware that you may have to evacuate – secure your home if told to leave.
- Listen and watch official media output.
- Local media news is likely to be more useful to you than national broadcasters.
- Only return home if told that it is safe to do so by the authorities.

RECOVERY

This is almost certain to take a long time, but the authorities will seek normality as soon as possible.

Safety at work

All places of employment should have an
emergency safety plan, with regular drills
to ensure that all employees are familiar
with it. If no such plan exists, find out why,
check with your union, and consult with
employers to institute a plan.

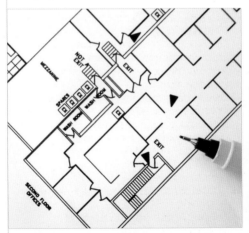

Know your workplace and plan your escape route.

Whether your workplace is located in a small unit or a large building, there should be a disaster survival kit in place (see pp 180–5).

PREPARATION

- Check that your company's reception always asks for ID.
- Ensure that your employer holds employees' next of kin details.
- Discuss the competence of IT security, virus protection, etc.
- Know your workplace and colleagues – note any strangers/suspicious behaviour.
- Trust your instincts – if anything is not as it should be, report it.
- Know the location of: emergency exits, fire extinguishers, first aid kit.
- Note anything out of the ordinary.
- Report any packages you think might be suspicious (see page 133).

RESPONSE

In the event of a terrorist incident, the top priority is safety.

- You may not have time to await official instructions.
- If in immediate danger, evacuate.

- Take the safest and quickest possible route out of the building.
- Once out, move as far away as possible from the building.
- Seek emergency service personnel.

RECOVERY

- Do not re-enter the building unless you are told that it is safe to so do by the emergency services on the scene.
- Take personal time to recover composure.
- Don't be afraid of seeking professional counselling after the event.

GENERAL ADVICE IN A TERRORIST SITUATION

- The key advice is to use: vigilance, awareness and common sense.
- Move away from any area or situation you are not comfortable with.
- Beware of unusual behaviour.
- Report anything suspicious to the authorities.
- Avoid places you do not know.
- Avoid back streets and secluded locations.
- Report furtive behaviour in anyone parking a car especially near a crowd or police station.
- Self-preservation is the order of the day.

Basic self-defence

The aim of self-defence is survival. Learn some basic techniques and you will be able to preserve your welfare, free yourself from constraint, and buy yourself enough time to run away.

All of us should have some knowledge of self-defence, and there are many institutions that offer formal instruction on how to defend yourself. Self-defence classes should also help equip you mentally for any physical struggle you might encounter.

Regular training in any martial art or self defence will not only teach you to survive, should the worst happen, but also help you develop the ability to overcome the 'rabbit in the headlights' syndrome. This instinct is one which readily translates to a disaster scenario.

The following pages feature basic techniques to help you to defend yourself, and offer advice for dealing with different scenarios in which you might be attacked by someone. They are designed, primarily, to help you to free yourself from your assailant. However, if an attacker does not leave the scene or does not allow you to, then it escalates into a struggle of a different nature altogether.

Two ways of escaping from an attacker.

If you are attacked by someone who is unarmed, from behind
- Grab the attacker's wrists and push down, squatting at the same time.
- Once free, jab your elbow sharply into the face of the attacker.

If your clothing or hair is grabbed
- Squat down – lowering your centre of gravity.
- Pull in your upper body.
- If freed from the attacker's grip, run.

If your hands are free
- Stab your attacker in the eye, making sure you combine your index and middle finger while doing so.
- Push your thumb into an eye.
- Try to break their grip by twisting their fingers or thumbs outwards.
- A sharp dig into their midriff with your elbow might release you (see above opposite).

If your arms have been pinned to your body
- Try a reverse head-butt – a sharp jerk of the back of your head into their face (see below opposite).
- Stamp your heel down forcefully on the attacker's foot.

If you are attacked from the front by an unarmed attacker

- Protect your throat by dropping your chin into your chest.
- Grab the attacker's thumbs and twist them away from your throat.
- Bring the butt of your hand up hard under his nose (see above opposite).

KNIFE ATTACKS

- An attacker with a knife has the advantage.
- If the knife attack is aimed downwards at your head, brace one clenched fist across the other to form a 'V' which will lock the stabbing action of the assailant's arm.
- A stabbing attack is more dangerous than slashing as it is more rapid.
- The best defence is to prevent the weapon being drawn.
- The next best defence is to put some distance between you and the attacker if you cannot rid him of the weapon.
- If a weapon alters the balance of power, try to equalise with a weapon of your own by improvisation – an umbrella, iron bar, chair, for example (see below opposite). Throw stones.

Using your hands, and using an everyday object as a weapon.

If your hair is grabbed, pulling your head downwards

- Punch sharply upwards into the attacker's jaw.
- If within reach, aim fingers or thumb for the attacker's eyes (a sharp jab).
- Use short, sharp punches into the genital region.
- Use a straight-fingered jab into windpipe.

If your arms are pinned to your body

- Try a head butt into the nasal region using your forehead.
- Bite their nose and mean it.
- Try to twist your assailant off balance and into the ground beneath you.
- If winded and they let go, run.
- Throw both of you against a wall or car, etc., with your attacker as the 'meat in the sandwich'.
- If you can get your attacker to fall beneath you, hitting the ground first, dig your elbow sharply into their ribcage.

If someone aims an upward kick at you

- Turn side on to them.
- Brace your non-standing leg.
- Turn that leg inwards and aim for their shin to connect with the sole of your foot.

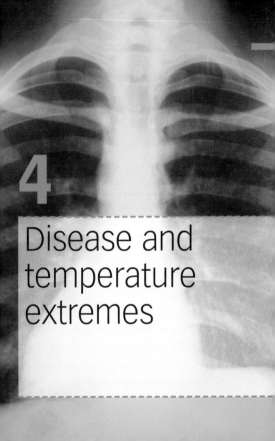

4

Disease and
temperature
extremes

Avian influenza

Although in excess of 200 cases of human infection have been confirmed since 1997, most avian influenza A viruses do not, as a rule, infect humans. This type of virus is usually highly species-specific and the virus cannot easily cross the species barrier. In recent years there have been just three instances of that barrier being bridged and that was the H5N1 virus. It is this variety which still presents the greatest risk of human infection because, given the right conditions, it has all the pre-requisites for starting another pandemic – except for one, and that is the ability to spread efficiently and sustainably amongst humans.

H5N1 principally results from human contact with infected birds, the main source of the virus, or contaminated surfaces – although there have been rare cases of human-human infection.

World health authorities are closely monitoring all of the outbreaks of human illness that are associated with avian influenza – this is because influenza A viruses have the potential for change and can therefore gain the ability to spread easily between humans.

PREPARATION

- Avian flu symptoms are similar to those of seasonal flu (see page 153).
- If there is any doubt or difficulty in determining which flu is present, always ensure that you consult a medical professional.

RESPONSE

- Consult a doctor.
- There are four anti-viral drugs (approved by the United States Food and Drug Administration) for the prevention and treatment of influenza, all four having activity against influenza A viruses: Amantadine; Rimantadine; Oseltamivir; Zanamavir.
- Practise effective hand hygiene and coughing etiquette (see page 154).

If you have to handle poultry

- Cooking destroys all germs, including bird flu viruses.
- Always wash your hands before and after handling poultry.
- Ensure that raw poultry is kept away from other foods.
- All utensils and surfaces must be kept clean.
- Using a food thermometer is the best way to

ensure that all food has been cooked to the safe internal temperature required.
• To be on the safe side, cook poultry to at least 73.9°C (165°F).

RECOVERY

In the UK, The Health Protection Agency advises anyone suspected of suffering from avian flu to stay home; sufferers might also be cared for in hospital, isolated from other patients for 7–10 days.

When handling raw poultry, keep all utensils and surfaces clean.

Pandemic flu

A pandemic is a disease that can spread globally, infecting vast numbers of people. Pandemic influenza occurs when a new strain of flu virus appears, to which people have not previously been exposed and therefore have no immunity. The major difference between pandemic and seasonal flu, which share similar symptoms, is that the latter is caused by virus types to which people have already been exposed thus its impact upon society is less severe, and vaccines, which are available, can limit the illness and its contagion.

Understanding the difference between seasonal flu and a pandemic is part of the crucial process of information and preparation.

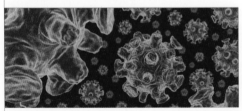

The influenza virus.

	SEASONAL FLU	PANDEMIC FLU
Causes	Viruses that are already circulating among the population.	Viruses to which people have previously *not* been exposed. More severe because of lack of immunity to the new virus.
Symptoms	Tiredness; runny nose; dry cough; muscle ache; headache. Fatalities can occur as a result of complications, such as pneumonia.	Similar to common flu but likely to be more severe with complications. Coughing may produce thick mucus; healthy adults may be prone to serious complications; acute breathing difficulties.

PREPARATION

A severe pandemic is a far greater threat to life than a seasonal flu outbreak. It can cause immense disruption to normal life because large numbers of people can fall ill at the same time. Being prepared and informed are two factors which can help reduce the impact of a pandemic. Adopt and follow good general health hygiene:

- Clean hands regularly with soap/cleansing agents.
- When you sneeze or cough, do so into a tissue that covers mouth and nose; cleanse hands afterwards and discard the tissue wisely.
- Help prevent germs entering the body by keeping hands away from eyes, nose and mouth.
- If signs of flu develop, stay away from work, school, and avoid contact with others.
- Ensure at least two weeks' supply of non-perishable food – supplies may be disrupted or you may just be unable to shop.
- Plan for any specific food needs – baby food, for example.
- Store water at the following rate: 4.5 l (1 gal) of water per person per day (two weeks' supply – half for drinking, half for food preparation/sanitation).
- Anti-flu vaccine may help you avoid seasonal flu – it will not prevent pandemic influenza.
- If over the age of 65, arrange a pneumonia vaccination to help prevent secondary infection.

RESPONSE

A flu virus is spread by contaminated droplets exiting the mouth or nose of an infected person and coming into contact with others.

- Ensure all family members' personal items are kept separate.
- Don't share – this applies to anything that needs to be touched to use (such as eating utensils or bars of soap).
- Regularly disinfect all commonly touched parts in the home – i.e. doorknobs, light switches, toilet hardware, etc.
- Wash hands after handling dirty laundry.
- If contact is likely with bodily fluids, wear disposable gloves.
- If caring for a sufferer, consider using a face mask.
- When washing hands, remember to scrub nails thoroughly.
- Use paper towels to dry hands; wipe taps with the same towel and then dispose of it (normal towels can spread infection).

RECOVERY
- Combat dehydration by taking plenty of liquids.
- Easily digestible food such as soup or broth should supplement liquid intake.
- Use medication, such as aspirin (or infant paracetamol for children), to reduce fever.
- Avoid alcohol or tobacco.
- A medical professional should be consulted, especially if home treatment doesn't help.

Hypothermia

Hypothermia occurs when the human body loses heat faster than it can replace it. When normal body temperature, 37°C (98.6°F), starts to drop, vital organs fail. Death occurs when the core temperature drops below 26°C (78°F).

The two types of hypothermia are acute and chronic. The former is caused by a sudden and total immersion in cold water, which can accelerate the loss of body heat more than 25 times quicker than cold air. Chronic hypothermia usually results from exposures of between 12 hours and several days.

As there are several levels of hypothermia, dependent upon subtleties of symptoms and body temperature, it is important to be able to distinguish between them and to apply appropriate treatment.

TREATMENT

If core body temperature drops below 35°C (95°F), proper medical help is required. If none is readily available, the following treatment should be given:

- Warm the victim up, slowly. The trunk of the body should be treated first.
- Do not apply warming to the extremities first – that will only drive cold blood to the heart and precipitate heart failure.

- Change the victim into dry clothing and wrap a blanket around their head and neck.
- Do not let the victim drink alcohol.

The stages of hypothermia

MILD HYPOTHERMIA (36°C /97°F and below)

Symptoms:

- Shivering.
- Cold extremities.
- Numbness.

Treatment:

- Avoid further heat loss and allow body to warm.
- Maintain warmth for several hours.
- Warm, sweet drinks – but NO alcohol or caffeine.

MODERATE HYPOTHERMIA (33°C /93°F and below)

Symptoms:

- Shivering may desist or even stop.

Treatment:

- Apply gentle heat.
- Give drinks, but only if the victim is conscious.

SEVERE HYPOTHERMIA (32°C /90°F and below)

Symptoms:

- Shivering may lessen or stop.
- Abnormal behaviour.
- Muscular rigidity.
- Victim may be conscious or semi-conscious.

Treatment:
- Handle victim with care.
- Lay them down on their back.
- Apply gentle heat.

CRITICAL HYPOTHERMIA (28°C /82°F and below)

Symptoms:
- Victim unconscious.
- Shallow or no apparent breathing/pulse.
- Blue/grey skin.
- Dilated pupils.

Treatment:
- Check carefully for signs of breathing and pulse for a couple of minutes.
- If the slightest sign of breathing or pulse, do not apply CPR.
- If no pulse/breathing, apply CPR (see page 175).
- Proper medical help is crucial as soon as possible.

Hyperthermia

The two most common forms of hyperthermia are heat exhaustion and heatstroke. The latter is more dangerous and requires immediate medical attention.

Beware exhausing expeditions in hot climes!

Hyperthermia occurs when the body's metabolic heat, or environmental heat load, exceeds normal heat-loss capacity or when there is impaired heat loss.

Heatstroke is a form of hyperthermia with accompanying physical and neurological symptoms. Heatstroke occurs when the body temperature rises to above 40ºC (104ºF). It can be fatal if not treated correctly and promptly. A dehydrated person may not be able to sweat fast enough to dissipate heat, leading to a rise in body temperature.

PREVENTION
Avoid over-activity in hot conditions, particularly when not in full health. Adequate fluid intake, before, during and after, is essential.

HEATSTROKE SYMPTOMS
- Breathing difficulties.
- Belligerence.
- Bizarre behaviour.
- Dizziness.
- Loss of balance.
- Strong and rapid pulse.
- Delirium.
- Fatigue.
- Dark urine usually an indicator.

RESPONSE

To treat heatstroke:

- Cool the victim down.
- Loosen clothing and ensure that the victim isn't overdressed.
- Get the victim out of the sun into a cool place, ideally air-conditioned, or shade.
- Removal to a cooler environment is not enough in itself to reverse internal heating. Whilst awaiting emergency medical aid, initiate measures to lower the body temperature. Use wet clothing, towels, icepacks, etc., to areas of greatest blood supply – groin, under arms, neck and knees.
- If possible, encourage the sufferer to shower, or bathe, or sponge down with tepid water.
- Offer fluids – preferably water and fruit juice (avoid alcohol and caffeine).
- Rest is essential.

HEAT EXHAUSTION SYMPTOMS

Symptoms are similar to those of heatstroke, though heat exhaustion is essentially a warning that the body is getting too hot.

- The victim may also suffer nausea.
- Skin is cold or clammy.
- Pulse may race.

RECOVERY
Heatstroke
- The most important measure in treating heatstroke victims is to counter dehydration by re-hydrating.
- Due to high internal temperatures produced by heatstroke, permanent damage to internal organs is possible.

Heat exhaustion
- Heat exhaustion recovery takes at least 24 hours of rest and re-hydration to reverse water deprivation.
- Full recovery from heat exhaustion is usually achieved within two days and is dependent upon age and general health.

Frostbite

Frostbite is the temporary or permanent skin tissue damage caused by prolonged exposure to temperatures of 0°C (32°F) and below. Exposed areas such as cheeks, ears, hands and feet are most susceptible. The skin freezes causing damage to the underlying blood vessels. It is possible to recover from frostbite if only the skin and tissues are damaged. The situation can become more serious if the blood vessels are damaged; gangrene can set in and amputation may be necessary.

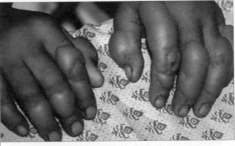

An example of badly frost-bitten fingers.

SYMPTOMS

- Goosebumps.
- Tingling sensation in the affected areas – skin can feel as if burnt.
- Partial or complete numbness – little or no feeling.
- Discolouration – pale or yellowish skin; the skin is cold.
- When thawing, the skin becomes painful and red.
- As the condition worsens pain begins to fade and eventually disappear.
- In severe cases, the affected skin turns black.

TREATMENT

- If possible, relocate to a relatively warmer environment.
- Re-warm affected area by placing in warm water (not too hot to touch) until the flesh softens and feeling becomes normal.
- Completely cover the damaged area with a bandage – sterile if possible – and warm clothing as well.
- Note: If it will not be possible to keep the thawed area from re-freezing, treatment should not be implemented as another bout of freezing can result in greater damage.

RECOVERY

- Proper medical aid should be sought as soon as possible.
- Because the outcome of frostbite injury cannot be predicted, at first all hospital treatment will follow a similar pattern, as detailed below.
- Aloe vera is applied to the affected area, which is then splinted, elevated and wrapped in a dressing.
- A tetanus shot – maybe penicillin – is used to prevent infection.
- The patient may require ibuprofen to combat inflammation.
- Drugs may be required in most cases to reduce high levels of pain that occur as sensation returns during warming.
- Treatment generally requires a hospital stay of several days.

5

Dealing with disasters

Psychological and emotional reactions to disaster

Experts agree that the timespan for recovery for those who survive a disaster depends on what they have endured and what meaning the victims gave to those events.

Cases of terrorist disaster can cause society to question their view of the world as a just and meaningful place and studies have shown that, as terrorism is premeditated, it creates a longer-lasting mental effect than natural disasters or accidents.

THE FIRST STAGE OF TREATMENT

Much of the initial mental health treatment in the immediate aftermath of a disaster has two primary goals:

- Normalise feelings – offering the victim reassurance that the strange and upsetting feelings experienced are normal, considering what they have been exposed to.
- Help victims find effective and acceptable ways of coping with ongoing stress.
- However unilateral a disaster may be, victims react in different ways and each case may need to be dealt with in a different manner.

Post-traumatic stress can affect emergency services workers.

The stages of disaster recovery

- Impact phase: response.
- Immediate post-disaster phase: survival.
- Recovery phase.

IMPACT PHASE

During this phase, individual behaviour is likely to be disorganised, with a certain degree of apathy.

Factors that trigger stress ('stressors') during this phase include:

- Threat to life.
- Inner feeling of helplessness.
- Loss – close family and friends.
- Dislocation from loved ones and familiar environment.
- Feelings of responsibility and wondering if more could have been done.

SURVIVAL PHASE

Signs that help is needed for post-traumatic stress disorder (PTSD):

- Difficulty in communicating thoughts.
- Troubled and disrupted sleep patterns.
- Flashbacks – reliving the trauma.
- Trouble maintaining balance.
- Anger.
- Sadness.
- Limited attention span.
- Mood swings.
- Propensity to cry easily.

RECOVERY PHASE

This phase commences once rescue is complete and individuals and communities face the task of restoring normality. It may include an element of disillusionment when the disaster no longer takes centre stage, leaving people to acclimatise to the reality of loss, etc.

There are many ways to help ease stress:

- Talking helps – share the feelings and emotions aroused, however difficult.
- Stay active and keep as near as possible to normal household schedule.
- Make quality time with family and friends.
- Reduce or limit physical and emotional demands that may be made on you.

SELF-HELP

In all cases of PTSD, professional help, diagnosis and treatment is crucial. However, there are also ways in which you can help yourself:

- Realise that your symptoms are not unusual given the circumstances.
- Follow your normal routine, even if the situation is not normal.
- Try to face, and resolve, any normal life obstacles that emerge – there is no need for you to add to the stress.
- Front any situations that may resurrect the trauma suffered.
- Know you cannot handle or control everything.

Basic first aid

Basic first aid is an 'on-site' response to any injury in the event of disaster and is not a substitute for professional medical help, which should be sought as soon as possible thereafter. These temporary measures should help a victim until they can receive qualified medical help.

All good first aid kits should have an instruction booklet or similar information to apply treatment.

This advice is given on the basis of four Bs: Breathing, Bleeding, Broken limbs and Burns.

BREATHING

This is the most important thing to check. If the patient is not breathing, this has to be restored before anything else is undertaken.

- If the patient is breathing but unconscious, place in the recovery position (see opposite) to prevent choking if vomiting occurs.
- If the patient isn't breathing – tilt head back and check throat for any blockage. Use a finger carefully to remove any obstruction.
- Pinch the patient's nose to close nostrils.
- Place a handkerchief or thin cloth over the patient's mouth and clamp your mouth to

completely cover the patient's mouth.
- Breathe deep and blow for a couple of seconds until you know that the patient's chest is rising.
- Pull back, let chest fall, and repeat the process.
- Listen for breathing and check pulse.
- If there is a pulse, apply 10 breaths per minute and continue until breathing is restored or help arrives.
- If there is no pulse, apply CPR (see page 175).

RECOVERY POSITION

Move the arm and leg on one side outwards to stop the injured person lying flat on the ground. Then bend the elbow and the knee. Turn the head in the same direction. Lay the other arm along the other side of the patient and let the other leg bend slightly.

The recovery position.

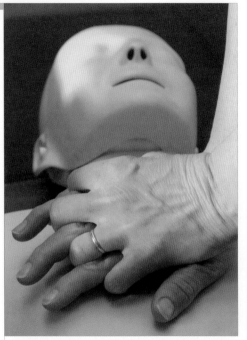

Clasp one hand over the other when giving CPR.

CARDIOPULMONARY RESUSCITATION (CPR)

If a victim's heart has stopped, CPR – which combines chest compressions with rescue breathing – can maintain oxygenated blood flow to the brain.

- Clasp one of your hands over the other.
- Place heel of lower hand 4 cm (1.5 in) from the end of the sternum.
- Press firmly down and release.
- Repeat at a compression rate of approximately 80 per minute – count 1000 and 1, 1000 and 2, and so on.
- Check for pulse.
- After 15 compressions, apply two breaths of mouth-to-mouth breathing.
- Repeat until pulse is restored, assistance arrives, or you are too exhausted. Rest, then repeat if necessary.

BLEEDING

If a wound is severe, bleeding to death is a distinct possibility. Arresting or slowing down blood loss may help a victim survive until professional help arrives.

- Push the edges of the wound together – if possible, secure the join with tape (duct tape, insulation tape, masking tape or anything similar).
- If a foreign body is imbedded in a major artery

DO NOT REMOVE; push the skin edges against it and bandage around the object.

- If a bandage is unavailable, use anything – be it an oily rag or dirty cloth; blood infection can be treated with antibiotics if the victim survives.
- Make sure that the victim is comfortable – lie them down and elevate the injured limb.
- Apply pressure to wound until bleeding ceases.
- If available, apply a sterile dressing. If not, urine can sterilise. Pad the dressing all round the foreign body.
- Check bandaging isn't too tight – press a finger or toenail. If the colour fails to return, loosen the dressing.

Cleaning wounds

If bleeding isn't too severe, cleaning a wound can prevent gangrene.

- Wipe the wound with antiseptic on cloth or cotton wool and dispose.
- Then wipe the wound again with fresh material, in the opposite direction.
- Apply dressing.

BROKEN LIMBS

First, try and alleviate the trauma of a broken limb by calming the victim.

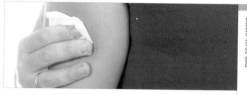

Apply pressure until bleeding stops.

- Don't move victim unless necessary for prevention of further injury.
- Dress any wound before splinting.
- Primary concern is to stabilise the broken limb without restricting circulation.

Broken legs

- If there is no wood or similar, brace the injured leg to the good leg; place padding between the ankles and knees and above/below break.
- Rolled up magazines can also be used (see page 178); clothing/folded blanket can form a 'soft splint'.
- Securing knots should be located on good leg.
- Apply an ice pack if available, but wrap in cloth – never apply to naked skin.
- If a stretcher is needed, improvise by pushing poles through arms of jackets or trouser legs.

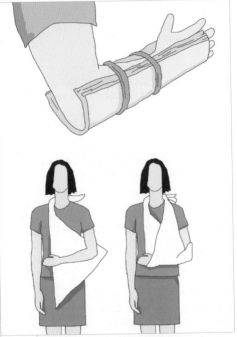

A makeshift splint and a triangular bandage for a sling.

Test before use, then roll the victim onto their side, place stretcher alongside, then roll the victim onto the stretcher.

Broken arms

- Support the arm in a triangular bandage, tied behind the neck (see below opposite). Weight should be carried at the elbow, which is held close to the upper body.
- Place padding between bandage and neck to prevent rubbing.
- If the break is near the elbow and the pain too severe, bandage arm to trunk of body. Place padding between arm and upper body for comfort.

BURNS

- Severe burns should be run under cold water – for at least 10 minutes or until the pain subsides.
- Remove any jewellery near the burnt area unless stuck to affected area. Do not break blisters.
- Try to make the victim as comfortable as possible.
- Burns should be covered with clean material to prevent infection. If suitable cotton fabric unavailable use plastic bag or cling film.
- Do not use adhesive dressings on burns.
- Seek medical help if you are in any doubt about the extent of the burn or how to deal with it.

Survival kits

Anyone who is unfortunate enough to be involved in any of the disaster scenarios featured in this book cannot know in advance when or where it will take place. However, most of the time most people will either be at home, at work, or travelling, either by car or public transport. The scale of a survival kit will depend on where it is located. A home survival kit is likely to be comprehensive, a work survival kit may be smaller but have greater quantity, in terms of consumables, dependent upon the number of staff it must provide for. A survival kit carried in a car may vary in size depending on how many people will usually use the vehicle.

HOME SURVIVAL KIT
Every kit should contain a basic first aid kit and a first aid booklet.

The first aid kit
This should contain the following items:
- Sterile adhesive bandaging – preferably rolls.
- Plasters of varying sizes.
- Triangular bandages.

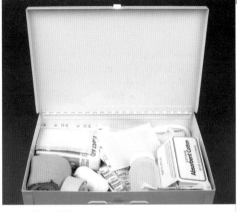

A typical first aid kit.

- Adhesive tape.
- Scissors – ideally, both small and large (with rounded ends).
- Tweezers.
- Sewing needles – small, medium and large.
- Antiseptic liquid, spray, or cream.
- Cotton wool balls.
- Cotton buds.
- Baby wipes – useful in water-shortage situations.

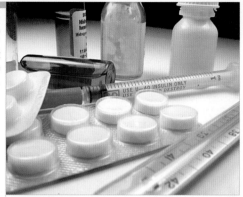

First aid kit items, including a syringe for diabetes sufferers.

- Thermometer.
- Petroleum jelly.
- Safety pins.
- Soap (liquid or solid).
- Surgical latex gloves.
- Sunscreen.
- Aspirin.
- Paracetamol or similar pain killer.
- Laxative.
- Anti-diarrhoea medicine.

Other items for your home survival kit

The home survival kit should also include emergency supplies, including:

- Radio – preferably wind-up to negate the need for batteries.
- A second radio with spare batteries.
- Torch/flashlight with spare batteries and bulbs.
- Water purification kit or tablets.
- Store of water (see page 184).
- Canned or dried food that doesn't need cooking.
- Tin opener – preferably non-electrical.
- Duct tape.
- Adjustable spanner/wrench.
- A multi-purpose pocket knife (Swiss army-type).
- String and rope.
- Any essential prescribed medication.
- Baby formula milk.
- Fire extinguisher.
- Large bin bags.
- Toothpaste.
- Feminine hygiene supplies.
- Toilet paper.
- Household bleach.
- Spare spectacles.
- ID.
- Cash.

SUPPLIES OF WATER

Guidelines as to the amount of water that should be stored varies, as does the duration that should be legislated for, but 2.27 l (4 pt) per person per day should be sufficient with the same again required for cooking and hygiene. Then multiply the amount by the number of people in a household. The final figure, for a three-day stay, should be multiplied by three. So, for example, a family of four would need 54.5 l (12 gal).

Plastic soft drinks bottles are good containers as they stack nicely, allowing a large quantity of water to be stored in manageable and accessible amounts. Such stores of water should be dated and the supply re-stocked every few months.

CAR SURVIVAL KIT

All cars should have a travelling survival kit. Any basic kit can be supplemented: for example, if snowstorms are expected add tyre chains.
The basic kit should include:

- Blanket or sleeping bag.
- Tool kit with adjustable spanners.
- Jump leads.
- Multi-purpose penknife.
- Bottled water – change regularly.

- Tinned fruit and food.
- Tin opener.
- Torch (with spare batteries and bulbs).
- Candles and matches.
- Extra clothing (waterproof).
- Spade.
- First aid kit.
- Duct tape.

It is very useful to carry a set of jump leads in your car.

Useful websites

Natural disasters
www.environment-
   agency.gov.uk
www.stormvideo.com
www.weather.com
www.weathereye.kgan.com
www.secretsofsurvival.com

Basic self-defence
www.self-defender.net
www.self-defense.info
www.selfdefense.org

Basic first aid
www.healthscout.com
www.netdoctor.co.uk
www.redcross.org

Man-made disasters
www.airtravelsurvival.com
www.emergency
   preparedness.org
www.travelnetscape.com
www.safety.com
www.wikihow.com
www.faa.gov
www.survive-nbc.org
   (terrorism)

Civil disasters
www.securityprousa.com
www.cdemcanterbury.
   govt.nz
www.ki4u.com

Anyone without internet access should visit their local library – most provide internet facilities. Your library may also have a selection of survival books and literature available to borrow.

In addition, it may have a range of information leaflets relating to disaster survival, or where specific literature may be obtained, such as the Home Office (United Kingdom).

Further reading

If you want to read more on the subject, here are a few suggested titles:

Bushcraft: An Inspirational Guide to Surviving the Wilderness by Ray Mears, Hodder & Stoughton Ltd (2002)

Emergency Disaster Survival Guide by Doug King, Acorn Publishers (1999)

Extreme Survival: What to Do When Disaster Strikes – In the Outdoors, the City and in the Home, How to Survive on Land, Water and in the Air, in Any Climate and Harsh Terrain by Bob Morrison, Harry Cook and Bill Mattos, Lorenz Books (2006)

Need to Know Outdoor Survival by John 'Lofty' Wiseman, HarperCollins (2006)

SAS Survival Handbook by John 'Lofty' Wiseman, HarperCollins (2003)

The Essential Survival Handbook by Ken Griffiths, Carlton Books Ltd (2002)

Index

Author acknowledgements

I wish to place on record my thanks to
the following:

My family, Bozenka, Ben, Sam and Jenny.

Steven Johnston, Black Belt and Karate
instructor KUGB.

Chris Mannix, Watch Manager, Cheshire Fire
and Rescue Service.

And I would like to dedicate this book to my Mam
and Dad, Gerald and Vera, with special thanks.

Photo credits

Page 76 © Peter Kneffel/epa/Corbis; page 126
© Reuters/Corbis; page 164 © Johan Copes Van
Hasselt/Sygma/Corbis